The God of Small Things

A Study in the Multiple Narratives

Arundhati Roy's

The God of Small Things

A Study in the Multiple Narratives

AÏDA BALVANNANADHAN

Prestige

an international publishing house

Published by
Prestige Books
3/28, East Patel Nagar
New Delhi 110 008
Ph. 9818755529
email: prestigebooks@gmail.com
website: asiabookclub.com
ISBN: 81-7551-193-1

Published 2007

Printed at Chaman Offset Press, New Delhi 110 002

Contents

Introduction

When one enters the magical world of *The God of Small Things*,[1] the powerful, poëtic prose overwhelms the senses. The lush vegetation of the quiet rural world of Ayemenem competes with the noisy and poor cities to impress itself upon the reader's mind. One can hear Estha's feet as he walks in the soaked earth. The main character, Rahel, very soon makes her appearance and guides us through this magical and yet terribly painful microcosm through her reminiscences. Once inside the narrative, we are overwhelmed by the twins' fear and helplessness, exhilarated by their minute childhood discoveries and suffer along with them in their final ordeal behind the History House and later at the police station. Even though the essence of the tragedy is told from the first chapter, the suspense is kept all along, thanks to the adroit rearranging of the events. The narrator drops small clues that do not make complete sense until the last tragic scenes, when the reader realises s/he has been told the entire story from the very beginning. All along the narrative, the narrator links the minute details of the tragedy to sub-stories that confer on the novel its dense quality. *The God of Small Things* tells more than one story and Roy has offered the novel to her readers[2] and the epigraph from the renowned writer, painter, and critic John Berger encourages the reader to search for other narratives behind the main one. The aim of this book is to try to share one of the many interpretations with the reader.

The chapters of the present study are arranged in a manner to follow the origin of the tragedy focusing on cause and effect, thus first focusing on the notion of hybridity with the twins as well as the relation of Ammu and Velutha. Then we move on in the second chapter to explain that inter-caste or inter-community sex is not prohibited or condemned in the same manner by the community in Ayemenem or India, depending on one's gender and caste. Consequently, Chacko can sexually exploit his female workers, while Ammu's marriage is frowned upon and eventually her sexual relationship with Velutha triggers off the tragedy. The third chapter reveals the situation of all the characters once they are caught in the clutches of history while at the same time tracing the narrator's constant time-shift which offers the hope of revealing the truth or at least another reading of this (his) story. This leads us to the fourth chapter which reveals that the narrative we read has been taken up by a woman, as in fact, behind the third person narrator, we have the perception of Rahel that colours the rendering of the tale. Finally chapter five shows us another aspect of power that had kept some characters imprisoned while it served others, and it is language, particularly the English language which is synonymous with power and social status. This final chapter gives an additional explanation to the lack of agency of certain characters in addition to their social belonging. The study is not and cannot be linear due to the myriad threads of meaning that send Roy's reader to and fro between the beginning and the end, between one voice or character and another, sometimes with just once word. Therefore the conclusion underlines the dense and polyphonic aspect of the novel which also comes from the various issues raised, and the groups that are given voice or at the least representation.

1. On the Author

(a) Extraordinary Beginnings

Suzanna Arundhati Roy was born on 24 November 1961. Her mother, Mary Roy, a Christian from Kerala, had been married to a Hindu tea planter and they had two children, Arundhati and her elder brother, Lalit. Arundhati Roy was born in Assam, Bengal, but following their mother's divorce and return to Ayemenem, the children had little contact with their father. Roy states she has seen her father only a couple of times and that she does not wish to discuss him.[3]

Considering the education she received, it is no wonder that Roy plays with language in the novel. She attended school only at the age of seven in her mother's informal school named Corpus Christi where learning was not a painful process sanctioned by exams, but rather a game, so to speak. The school's methods were such a success that the high-class families would register their yet to be born children in order to secure a place for them. Mary Roy is also famous for having changed the inheritance laws in Kerala, which now grant equal inheritance rights to Christian women.[4]

Apparently inheriting her social activist mother's combative spirit, Arundhati decided to leave home at the early age of sixteen in a society where parents still arrange their children's weddings to live her life as she intended. She lived in a squatter's camp in Ferozshah Kotla, Delhi, and sold empty beer bottles to support herself through her studies. She entered Delhi's School of Planning and Architecture and left without finishing her studies. She married Gerard Da Cunha, a fellow student and together they decided to live in Goa selling pastries, as neither had an interest in making a living off architecture. After four years the couple split as Arundhati had had enough of selling cakes and of tourists.[5] She then returned to Delhi where she chose to live supporting herself as an aerobics instructor after she met the film director Pradip Krishen who offered her a small role in *Maassey Saab*.[6] However, she obtained an eight-month scholarship to study the restoration of monuments in Italy when she had just started to know Krishen. She declares she discovered her talent for writing fiction while corresponding with Krishen from Italy.

Arundhati Roy is now married to Pradip Krishen. They live in New Delhi.

She wrote and co-starred in the film *In Which Annie Gives It to Those Ones* after her sojourn in Italy. In 1992, she wrote the script for the film *Electric Moon* and several television dramas followed. Two articles that lambasted Shekhar Kapur's film *Bandit Queen* as an exploitation of the life of the famous Indian female bandit, Phoolan Devi,[7] caused a controversy that interrupted her career as a promising script writer despite a devoted following. Roy even had to face a court case for her two columns against Kapur's film. Revolted, she retired from the film world and decided to concentrate wholly on the book she had already begun. She had apparently informed no one of her project, neither her mother, nor Pradip Krishen. In 1997, her book was ready after almost five years of work. Published during the summer, the book was an immediate success and was short-listed for the Booker Prize.

(b) Controversy

Roy was not new to controversy as her book was written after the storm about the film on Phoolan Devi, but her novel caused even greater controversy as no one had yet won the Booker with a first novel and moreover without having the credentials of the typical Commonwealth writer, educated in the West or in the best Indian institutions. Here was a person, who flitted from one interest to another, architecture, script-writing, socially-committed writing: her writer's CV was unusual, but her novel a small wonder. The novel was translated into more than forty languages in much less time than other literary 'hits.' Roy's book caused a great sensation on the literary arena when it was published. Praise as well as criticism flowed as is often the case with bestsellers.

Some of the literary world sulked and claimed her book was just a clever marketing product using the fame Salman Rushdie had given to India to 'sell' the subcontinent. Certain critics went to the extent of claiming that her novel was "derivative" as Rushdie had already "done India," thus revealing their prescriptive attitude on what writers should 'do' or what India has yet to offer to the world! In reality, interest and tourism in Kerala have revealed that it was Roy who brought her region under the spotlight by her novel. Former member of the Booker prize committee, Carmen Callil judged the book extremely negatively despite the international recognition it received, labelling it as "vulgar." Callil went to the extent of commenting upon the fellow-judges' decision to award this first novel the much-coveted Booker Prize as "an execrable decision." Lionised by some, reviled or even hated by others, Roy certainly disturbs and provokes strong emotions, particularly for her political writings, while her single novel had immediately interested the academic world mesmerised by her extremely fresh approach to language, as in *Arundhati Roy: The Novelist Extraordinary*, R.K. Dhawan's edition of articles by a large number of international scholars.[8]

On tour for the promotion of her book, Arundhati Roy was not informed of the storm that awaited her in her native land. In June 1997, a lawyer, Sabu Thomas filed a public interest petition on the grounds that the love scene couched in lyrical language in the last three pages of the novel was obscene and demanded that the pages be removed. Strangely, the petition did not mention the distressing scene describing child abuse in the middle of the book as M. Thomas worried only about the morality of the Indian readers considering the description of the love scene as immoral. What really disturbed was not the description of the lovemaking, which cannot be considered explicit, but rather the fact that it happened between a high-caste woman and an untouchable, for it must be said, the *Kama Sutra* is far more explicit in its treatment of sex than Roy's book. Arundhati Roy's novel threatened the almost undisturbed traditions of a hierarchical society where there are biological explanations to the status quo that has been existent for centuries. Her social activism concerning the Narmada dam project was the last drop.[9] Enough is enough, decided the State and after her first piece of non-fiction targeting the government, in which she gives a piece of her mind on the dam projects,[10] the author has been subjected to continual harassment by the highest institution of India, the Supreme Court. The harassment did not bend Roy's will for she has published other critical political essays, such as her contribution 'War is Peace' in a collection of essays by known figures such as Noam Chomsky and Harold Pinter on the US war on Afghanistan.[11]

Like Henry David Thoreau, Roy has stood up alone against the state. Like Thoreau, she has spent one night in prison, agonising on whether to pay a symbolic fine or to spend the next six months in gaol. The ludicrous trial for contempt of court Roy faced in 2001-2, caused an international scandal as support groups all over the world denounced the harassment to which the author had been subjected to since her first non-fictional prose, *The Greater Common Good* against the Indian government's dam projects came out in 1998. After Roy appeared very briefly to support the victims of the Narmada Dam Project, which will make thousands of citizens homeless without offering any compensation, she was accused of threatening a group of lawyers with death.[12] The hurriedly written complaint by a group of lawyers for Roy's 'menacing them with death,' inciting violence, and for 'behaving like a thug,' just as the legal proceedings of the Supreme Court, were seriously, severely, and of course wittily, criticised by the author in her affidavits and her latest publication.[13] However, when the Court's dignity could have been saved by a retreat from such obvious and shameful persecution that is unworthy of representatives of law, therefore repairing India's reputation abroad, matters actually worsened. Indeed, the country's reputation as a democracy seemed to matter less to her persecutors than the maintenance of the 'dignity' of the Supreme Court, dignity, apparently viewed in a different manner by Roy and the members of the Supreme Court themselves. The Supreme Court that would usually take months to hear a case, actually hurried through the procedures in order to have Roy in court. When the Court went to the extent of closing its doors to journalists, whilst other members, hostile to Roy, were allowed in and were not punished even though they did not respect the 'solemnity' of the court, the intentions of her persecutors became increasingly plain. The Supreme Court itself was, in a sense, going against the law in its obvious attempt to frighten and bully Roy by preventing her from having any support or even witnesses in the court. The Supreme Court of India had only managed to ridicule itself on the international scene by its very attempt to have its 'dignity' respected.

The thousands of fans expecting another novel from the author of *The God of Small Things* will have to be patient. Roy's time is taken up as she has two battles in progress, supporting the oppressed poor classes in their struggle for their land threatened by the dam projects and her own against the highest representatives of the country.[14]

Concerning International politics, she has spoken out against the USA's military interventions in Afghanistan and in Iraq.

2. The Background to *The God of Small Things*

(a) Kerala: From Matriarchy to 20th Century Feminism

Kerala, one of the smallest states in the Republic of India, was formed in 1956. It is situated along the Malabar Coast, on the western side of the Indian peninsula. It is bordered by the states of Karnataka on the north, Tamil Nadu to the east and the Arabian Sea on the west.

The Communist Party of India was founded in the second decade of the last century. In 1957, one year after the state of Kerala was formed, it became the first state in the world to form a democratically elected communist government. In 1970, Kerala became the first state in India to abolish landlordism. The period between these two dates was not a peaceful one and Roy's description of the violent demonstrations in 1969 is hardly a fictionalisation of reality. The violent struggles and the deaths of leaders like Charu Mazumdar, communist revolutionary and initiator of the Naxalbari trend, before he was killed in the custody of the Indian state in 1972, were in vain, for the caste divide was too deep to rally the people into one unified group with a clearly defined political aim. Kerala is presently a democratic state, and is still under Marxist control.

Concerning gender issues, the position of women in Kerala had been much higher before the influence of the British who changed certain laws[15] as they considered the matriarchal structure of the Hindu society in Kerala morally unacceptable.

> In Kerala, despite their loud avowals that there would be no interference in personal law, the imperial state intervened quite blatantly to recast the matrilineal Nair *taravads* (households) into what they spoke of as a "natural" patriarchal mould. [. . .] Taravad land was subject to matrilineal inheritance, but was held by all in common and administered by the eldest brother; women were free to cohabit with other (usually Namboodiri Brahmin) men, but no rights were attached to these sambandhams. In a series of Nair Regulation Laws, starting in 1868 and continuing well into the 1930s, this form of family organization, which gave a woman economic power and sexual freedom or, in the phrasing of the Marriage Commission, the right to terminate a union 'at any time, from wantonness or caprice,' was brought to heel.[16]

This same British interference influenced the cultural life in India. The anglicised nationalists of the period were only promoting puritan Victorian values. Further into India's past, some women were in a prominent position and certain arts such as *Naach*, temple dancing, were not considered licentious by the Indians as by the British who erased this social group of women by the promotion of laws against the *naach* or dance. Women's writing also underwent Victorian censure. Tharu and Lalitha evoke the savage editing of the sexually explicit verses of the sensual poems of *Muddupalani, Radhika Santwanam* by the British or those who integrated Victorian notions of propriety.

> In 1887, these works were trimmed and recast. [. . .] They excised not only the verses they considered sexually explicit or obscene but also the peetika, or colophon, in which the woman writer traced her female lineage and spoke with confidence, unusual for later times, about her achievement as an artist.[17]

The Kerala that is described in the novel has in fact regressed in certain aspects, as women seemed to enjoy more freedom and more legal rights in certain cases before British intervention. Indeed, as Meenakshi Mukherjee points out, this English influence on Indian novelists' publications was a result of their vision of what a proper education was meant to be. "This was consistent with the other effect of English education, namely the desire to reform Hindu society or at least to purge it of its excesses."[18] In fact, Roy seems to comment on the changes that pushed woman lower in the social sphere through Ammu's comment in the novel that a woman hadn't much choice when she had to choose between her father's and her husband's name; a strong reminder surely of Kerala's past matrilineal society.

Roy's book can thus be considered as being in the lineage of the older, Indian, female literary tradition, where the pride of achievement can make sense despite the court case against her for obscenity. In a state where communism has been a factor in the higher education of its population, women included, and where simultaneously the effects of the *Bhadralok* upbringing of the women are strong, a female author who earns the Booker Prize with a début novel and is at the same time accused of obscenity can hardly surprise.

(b) 'Keralese' or the Exoticism of Indian-English Writing

Despite the academic term "New Literatures in English" that purports to include most writings in English of former English colonies, in reality, Indo-Anglian[19] writing is not that recent. It goes back to the nineteenth century when it began mostly with poetry of which the most renowned are given here in chronological order. At the earliest stage we find Michael Madhusudana Datta (1824-1873), who wrote a long poem, *The Captive Lady* (1849), and Henry Louis Vivian Derozio (1809-1831), whose most well known poetic work is The *Fakir of Jungheera.*

Kerala itself was already present on the literary scene with Chandu Menon's *Indulekha* 1889). This places Arundhati Roy in a centenary heritage as R.K. Dhawan points out.[20]

At the end of the nineteenth century, even women's writing in English was beginning to receive recognition. The poetess Toru Dutt, whose novel, *Bianca or the Young Spanish Maiden* published in 1878, was calqued on Samuel Richardson's *Pamela.* Among the most renowned are the poetess called 'India's Nightingale,' Sarojini Naidu of whose works are the following: *The Golden Threshold* (1905), *The Bird of Time* (1912), and *The Broken Wing* (1917) and the Noble Prize-winner Rabindranath Tagore (1861-1941). Tagore, who wrote both in English and in Bengali and translated some of his own works, is a major figure of Indian poetry. Among Tagore's works are the English version of *Gitanjali*, a volume of 103 poems, published in 1910 and translated into English in 1912, and *The Home and the World* (1916).

The novel is set in the nationalist period, and reflects the national sentiment of the Swadeshi movement of boycotting British goods after the first partitioning of Bengal by Lord Curzon's government.

During the nationalist movement, Indian-English writing took on a different aspect as fictional and non-fictional works mostly dealt with the social effects of colonisation and reflected the political activism of the period. It is only after independence that the writers started turning inwards to examine the Indian society or to treat individual subjects.

Today Indian writing is long established on the international scene with names such as Raja Rao, Mulk Raj Anand, and R.K. Narayan, which gave India its prominent place on the international literary scene since the 1930s. More recently, Indian writers have settled abroad being invited to lecture in foreign universities either due to international recognition in other cases, or regarding their personal lives, like Anita Desai, Amitav Ghosh, Kamala Markandaya and Salman Rushdie, to mention but a few. Arundhati Roy has been made various offers, some serious, others frivolous and has refused them in order to remain anchored in India where she is leading social struggles as for example for the rights of those made homeless by the Narmada project.

Concerning the exoticism of Indian writing in English, from the very beginning, it has received a cool response if not severe criticism, mostly from Indian critics who see in it a continuation of Thomas Macaulay's 'Minute on Education' which advocates the moulding of the Indian mind through the education of a selected few in the English language so as to serve the English interests.

> Various objections immediately arise; these poets are city poets (Calcutta, Madras, Bombay, Delhi), their awareness of life is attached to an artificial wavelength of superficial cosmopolitanism and sophistication, which alienates from what are known as the masses; their responses are conditioned by school and college readings of Odes to Nightingales . . . : they write in a language against which the vernacular literary establishments are solidly ranged; they have no real public, and are therefore doomed to the limbo of neglect from English and American poets and faulty appreciation from the Indians; they are rootless, colourless, money-plants, hanging out leafy tongues in despair.[21]

Yet, Raja Rao's preface to his own novel *Kanthapura* should have put an end to the debate on the use of the English language. The debate is still raging today to a certain extent due to the conflicting relations English writing has with the literatures of the 'regional languages.' However recently, literature in regional languages is more widely diffused and its translation into the English language makes it known even on an international level. For Rao, it is clear that English that has become an Indian 'dialect' in a way.

> We cannot write like the English. We should not. We can only write as Indians. We have grown to look at the large world as part of us. Our method of expression therefore has to be a dialect which will be as distinctive or as colourful as the Irish or the American.[22]

Roy indeed writes in an English that is not only Indian, but that she has made hers, adapting it to the needs of her novel, and its characters from Ayemenem. She certainly does not seem to have written her novel to satisfy the Western reader with his/her vague image of India, an attitude that is exemplified by Miss Mitten's notion that people spoke 'Keralese' in Kerala. As Corrado Micheli points out in his article, the Macaulay project was turned on its face as under-evaluation of Indian writers or Indian English is most certainly anachronistic today with the success of Indian writers in Anglophone countries.[23] She does not go out of her way to explain words or events, but just gives some hints as might be necessary even to a native considering the number of languages spoken in the subcontinent. Of course, even today the vicious attack by P. Lal against Indian-English writers for their base, venal aims is existent as many writers are accused of writing with a Western audience in mind. But in a country where there are more than a hundred languages and dialects, where marriage customs, food and vestmental habits differ so widely even within a distance of less than a hundred miles, writing in the English language and even adding a glossary at the end of a novel is only natural.

> While the basic ideas of life do have an all India character, the regional life cannot be the same. How much of a south Indian Iyengar family is understood if some of their customs and culinary practices are not described? [24]

To terminate a discussion which risks giving more importance to ideology than to creativity, one can say that what counts is not the language or the themes the author uses or treats, but the artistic quality of the work. It is not for critics to prescribe what an artist should write, which subjects or languages the artist should avoid, for in this lies the danger of curbing inspiration and muzzling the mind. Indian writing in English has survived years of controversy and is well established. It is so fixed and successful that some budding authors even in the West emulate it.[25] Indeed not only do some feel it necessary to use Indian characters and themes in their writing because India is a subject that sells, but the emulation goes to the extent of following a typical bakery recipe. Incorporate a smattering of Indian history, a dash of the famous fanaticism vs. freedom of expression through allusion to a well-known book, a smidgen of the Salman Rushdie style or metaphors, a wee bit of Arundhati Roy and the cake is baked. Are we in the midst of one of those moments in history where literary styles are invented by great authors to set a trend or are we in the midst of a clever marketing era? It is difficult to tell but one can clearly state that Indian writing in English is not a passing fad.

This is the complex background to Roy's first novel which in itself is a dense polyphonic world with several layers of narratives of which it is the humble aim of this book to trace but a few.

NOTES

1. *The God of Small Things* (London: Flamingo, 1997).
2. "When I write, I lay down my weapons and give the book to the reader." See Internet pages http://www.salon.com/sept97/00roy.html *The Salon Interview* with Reena Jana, 30 September 1997.
3. '"I don't want to discuss my father. I don't know him at all. I've only seen him a couple of times, that's it," she told Sunday Plus when pressed.' See Internet page http://website.lineone.net/~jon.simmons/roy/tgodt6c.htm .
4. See George Iype's interview of Mary Roy on Internet page http: // www.rediff.com/news/sep/18arun.html *The Rediff Special* by George Iype.
5. See Internet page http://website.lineone.net/~jon.simmons/roy/tgod 6c. htm .
6. *Ibid.*
7. Arundhati Roy, *The Great Indian Rape Trick*, I, August 22, 1994 and *The Great Indian Rape Trick* II, September 3, 1994.
8. R.K. Dhawan, *Arundhati Roy: The Novelist Extraordinary* (New Delhi: Prestige, 1999).
9. Arundhati Roy's struggle against the building of dams in the Narmada Valley started with her essay 'The Greater Common Good' in *The Cost of Living* (London: Flamingo, 1999). This activism of the author for the rights of those that the dam projects will make homeless has led to her harassment by the Supreme Court of India despite international support, see her recent book, *Power Politics* (Cambridge, Massachusetts: South End Press, 2001). See also Internet pages, http://www.geocities.com/~dvadi/articles/aroy_dbars.html for 'Arundhati Roy The Progressive Interview' by David Barsamian, and http://www.narmada.org/articles/arinterview.html for 'Arundhati Roy in conversation with Venu Govindu,' Oct. 29, 2000 at the NBA Dharna in Bhopal. Roy's other struggle is a lawsuit filed against her for obscenity by Sabu Thomas because of the lyrical description of the love scene between Ammu and her Untouchable lover, see Internet page http://www.salon.com/sept97/00roy.html 'The Salon Interview' by Reena Jana, Sept. 30, 1997.

10. Arundhati Roy, *The Cost of Living.*
11. Ken Coates, ed. *War is Peace. The Spokesman* (N) 73. (Nottingham, UK: Russell Press, 2001).
12. See Internet page http://www.geocities.com/~dvadi/articles/aroydbars.html for David Barsamian's *The Progressive Interview.*
13. See chapter 'On Citizens' Right to Express Dissent' in Arundhati Roy, *Power Politics.*
14. For more details on the whole case and a reading of Roy's affidavits and imprisonment, see Internet pages on http://www.narmada.org/sc.contempt, http://books.guardian.co.uk/news/articles.
15. *Report of the Malabar Marriage Commission with Enclosures and Appendixes* (Madras: Government Printers, 1891). Qtd. Susie Tharu and K. Lalitha, *Women Writing in India. 600 B.C. to the Present* (Delhi: Oxford University Press, 1995), Vol. I, p. 159.
16. Susie Tharu and K. Lalitha, Vol. I, p. 159.
17. *Ibid.*, Vol. II, p. 11.
18. Meenakshi Mukherjee, *Realism and Reality, The Novel and Society in India* (Delhi: Oxford University Press, 1985), Chap. 2.
19. Critics have created several terms to describe writing linked to India as a subject and this particular term designates writing in English produced by Indian authors.
20. R.K. Dhawan, Introduction.
21. P. Lal, ed., "Indian Writing in English: A Reply to Mr. Jyotirmoy Datta," *Quest*, 1964. Ten Years of Quest, 1966. Qtd. G. Aswathanarayana Reddy, *Indian Writing in English and its Audience* (Bareilly: Prakash, 1979), pp. 4-5.
22. Raja Rao, Preface to *Kanthapura* (1938; New York: New Directions, 1963), p. vii.
23. Corrado Micheli, "The Eccentric Voice of *The God of Small Things*," in Dhawan, ed., *Arundhati Roy: The Novelist Extraordinary.*
24. G. Aswathanarayana Reddy, p. 63.
25. Zadie Smith's *White Teeth* contains passages where the imprint of *The God of Small Things* is clearly visible, such as the 'angry feelings that rise from the shoes.'

Chapter I

Hybridity

Hybridity is an essential theme in the novel, as it is one of the major factors that lead to the tragedy of the twins and their mother. However, hybridity is not always a factor of social condemnation, as the elements of the "crossing" can count as socially elevating in certain cases. Undeniably, Ammu's inter-religious marriage places her twins in a lower position, even though the same logic is not applied in relation to Sophie Mol, issue of an "inter-racial" marriage. In the *Manavadharmashastra*,[1] a book of Hindu precepts, a man who marries a woman belonging to a lower caste elevates her, while the contrary is not true as the woman loses her caste. There is a possibility of the creation of yet another hybrid child due to the sexual relations that Ammu has with Velutha. Velutha is an untouchable and this relation is therefore perceived as a threat to the social order as we shall discuss it later. Therefore, hybridity in the novel is elevating or marginalizing, depending on historical, economic and gender factors.

1. Mixed Marriages

Though Estha is only seven, he realises that as Rahel and he are offsprings of an inter-religious, inter-community, love marriage they are in a position of weakness and perhaps even on the margins of society as they are considered hybrid children. Rahel's anxiousness to verify if her uncle Chacko loves her despite his daughter's imminent arrival is reflected in Estha's additions to the songs sung by Julie Andrews in "The Sound of Music." In

Estha's version, the white couple will not include brown children in their home. The lack of paternal love that they suffer from, leads to the twins' perpetual search of a father figure. Their uncle's rejection of them—symbolically heightened by his refusal of their adding any appellation that holds in it a family connection when they call him uncle—leads to a doubled anxiety felt by the twins between the reality of the family and their position in society in the historical context. This anxiety entails from their uncle pointing to the fact that as a high-caste family they are cast-offs of history in relation to India's colonial past. The twins are indeed high-caste children but are of an inferior breed that the Indian system does not wholly recognise. The case of Estha and Rahel resembles that of Chacko's own daughter who is a hybrid product of two systems, races and classes. Both Chacko and Ammu defied the social order by marrying out of their caste or group and pay for it by the collapse of their marriages. As Hanquart-Turner Evelyne points out, failure, even death is the outcome of interracial marriages and there is a continuation of this theme in Roy's novel.[2] Thus even the children pay for their parents' illusions of successfully transgressing the existent divisions, between 'race' (black and white) as in the case of Margaret and Chacko; of religion and community as in the case of Ammu and her husband. The consequences are that the twins' lives are shattered and Sophie Mol dies a violent death.

Pappachi whose entrance into Western society is aborted, as his name is not recognised as the discoverer of the moth, passes on this failure to his descendants, the moth becoming a kind of symbolic "curse." All the family is affected by this failure and even Sophie Mol's death is pre-shadowed through the image of the moth, when the conversation circles "like a moth" around her. The outcome of hybridity, especially when it is the interaction between the West and the East, is always negative.

(a) Pollution in Miscegenation versus Inbreeding Madness

Those affected by the violent struggle between the two sexes in the novel are the children and the women themselves even when it is paradoxically the women who undertake violent actions. Women and children, who are equally vulnerable, reap the bitter harvest of miscegenation. The women are bound to an immutable tradition that places them in an a-historical position as regards their social status and rights, contradictory to their reality of strong nurturing figures. This stasis is what obsesses Rahel, for her struggle is against time that has buried her brother's painful memories, petrifying his mind and her life as they have "joint identities" (2). The times of their childhood memories such as the precious moments of joy and other terrible ones have been recorded by Rahel's toy watch on which time is painted as a metaphor of their helplessness in the face of History, and the phrases, "Ten to Two," "Lay Ter," "Dum Dum," an objective correlative of time as a dreaded enemy.

The helplessness of the twins is mastered by the constant shift in time between Rahel who casts about for ways in which to bring her alienated brother back to his mind, and the dynamism of her shifting thoughts which hold in them Estha's now probable liberation from guilt as they share the same thoughts. Rahel's exhumation of Estha's notebook and child's tale is indeed the starting point to unveiling his long-blinded memory so that he can at last reap the relief of grief to move towards an irenic acceptation of his terrible but forced role as traitor on Velutha's ignominious end. Rahel helps her twin brother to reap lost innocence, by making him realise that he was an object in Baby Kochamma's scheme and not a guilty subject. This is reflected in the hideous grief the twins share.

Woman's labour is rewarded by loss, as we know that Ammu has not received a share in her parents' factory. Like all divorcees, and particularly one who is married to someone from a different religion and through her own initiative, she lives on sufferance with her children in the Ayememen home as the cook informs the children, "Tell your mother . . . This isn't your house" (83), all this, despite Ammu's hard work in the pickling: "Though Ammu did as much work . . . because Ammu, as a daughter, had no claim to the property" (57). Little wonder then, that Ammu refuses to choose either her father or her husband's name.

The only other male who loses all is named in Ammu's dream as the "God of Loss." He is savagely emasculated by the police both in an act of jealousy for his having had a sexual relationship with a high-caste woman, as well as a means of dissuasion for all Untouchables, for the mere potentiality of a hybrid child this short relationship has in it, "And a history lesson for future offenders" (336), the offence being the merging with the hated, the feared or the despised Other. As Bhabha remarks: "The paranoid threat from the hybrid is finally uncontainable because it breaks down the symmetry and duality of self/other, inside/outside."[3]

The homes of the upper caste families are guarded as temples, to which the supposedly polluting Untouchables have no access. Indeed, with local idiosyncrasy, even Christianity had been adapted to the caste-system as the Untouchables have a separate church from the higher classes. "When the British . . . separate Pariah Bishop" (74). It is the hypocrisy of the system that makes Mammachi allow Velutha enter the house when she needs something mended or installed (77) while she believes all the while that his touch pollutes. Killing Velutha is not understood by the members of the community as an act of violent battle but as a medical precaution, not very surprising when orthodox Brahmins employing Untouchables are known to sprinkle water over their dishes after the untouchable servant has cleaned them! This explains the "sober, steady brutality" (308) of eliminating Velutha, as "merely inoculating a community against an outbreak" (309).

The house will later be almost barricaded by an ageing Baby Kochamma, so terrorised at the idea of being robbed that she hardly opens her windows. Her continual watching of television revives her fears of the Communist revolution (28) that would have theoretically wiped out the caste differences. Ironically, even the exploitation of the gifted Paravan for lower fees than a member of a higher caste becomes a social promotion in the eyes of the 'Modalali,' Mammachi: "She said it was a big step for a Paravan" (77), that is, to enter the home of a high-caste even if it is only as a servant.

Ammu's body, as belonging to the rest of the high caste, is also to be fiercely guarded. Ammu cannot mother the son of an Untouchable in the society described, for even her twins, hybrid issues of an intercommunity love marriage, are regarded as a menace to the equilibrium of a country deeply entrenched in its age-old system of divisions. This is why the narrator significantly uses the verb "enter" to reveal the sacrilegious nature of Velutha's act. Velutha polluted a high-caste womb, and in that act did lay the possibility of the procreation of a half-caste child that would wreak havoc in the structure of the society that supposes the purity of the high-caste groups. This myth is shared by most societies that found their hierarchical structure on the idea of the purity of the ruling classes. Velutha's lovemaking with Ammu had in it at least the hypothetic possibility of a child being born, therefore this second and even graver possibility of miscegenation which no longer concerns an intercommunity love marriage, but an inter-caste sexual relationship cannot be allowed to produce a new type of 'hybrid' that would destroy the social order and hierarchy maintained for centuries. Velutha's sowing can only result in reaping a violent annihilation for both himself and Ammu by the guardians of this order and their particular narration of 'History.' A group who fervently believe in the purity of their group(s), will turn to fanaticism when other versions of history which reveal their hybridisation, as explains the French psychoanalyst, Daniel Sibony.[4] This supposed purity of the peoples of India from the Vedic times, in particular the high-caste groups, is what makes Ammu's and Velutha's act reprehensible. I say 'supposed' as in fact Manu has already alluded to deviations by commenting on the consequences of this kind of miscegenation. A man from a higher caste does not alter the purity of the offspring by marrying a woman of a lower caste while the contrary situation will alter the purity of the race. The miscegenation exists then, historically proved and recorded, except that one form of it is accepted and the other made reprehensible, in the patriarchal system of Hinduism. This explains Vellya Paapen's terror at witnessing what he considers a violation of sacred laws. "Not until he saw what his Untouchable son had touched. More than touched. Entered. Loved" (78). Indeed Baby Kochamma quotes the Bible to justify Velutha's savage murder as a divine retribution. "As ye sow, so shall ye reap" (31). The narrator's comment, "As though she had nothing to do with the Sowing and Reaping" (31), underlines the presence of the human hand in the tragedies, of which the criminal results are presented as celestial intervention.

Miscegenation is punished, not by secular law, but by man-made law rendered divine, that is, crystallised in religion. It is religion that forbids the mixing of the white-skinned or at least fair-skinned Brahmins with the dark Untouchables. However, Roy's lyrical description of the scene of lovemaking between the lovers holds in it the criticism of unnatural man-made laws that interfere with the very course of nature which is placed above laws. The act of lovemaking is described as a dance designed by nature, "Biology designed the dance," (335) thus questioning the laws that forbid the union of the lovers. The lovers' teasing of each other when they dispose of very little liberty or time is similar to two birds or two animals' love parade. The knowledge of the religious laws that forbade such a biological 'mating' is what raises the stakes of their act. Therefore, it is understandable that when Velutha's very human constitution and condition make him fall in love with Ammu or at least desire her, the timing of his act becomes dictated by the terror of punishment, leaving the lovers hardly any time to savour their forbidden love. "Terror timed it" (335). Man-made history overpowers biology.

Ammu and Velutha's living their passion so intensely comes from their knowledge that their hopes for a happy future are as fragile as the lives of a spider, they baptise Chappu Thamburam, Lord Rubbish. "(T)hey linked their fates, their futures their Love, their Madness, their Hope, their Infinite Joy to his. [. . .] They chose him because they knew they had to put their faith in frailty. Stick to Smallness." (339) Yet, placing the promise of the lovers' encounter at the very end of the novel while it is not the chronological end of the tale, might suggest that the smaller pleasures of life are worth transgressing the rules, for indeed Ammu confirms to her anxious son Estha, that even a dream counts.

> 'If you're happy in a dream, Ammu, does that count?' Estha asked. 'Does what count?' 'The happiness—does it count?' She knew exactly what he meant, her son with his spoiled puff. Because the truth is, that only what counts counts. (218)

Therefore, considering the fact that the narrator relates the tale through the vision of an adult Rahel, one can say that the aim of the novel is indeed celebration of love, and of the little pleasures despite its treatment of a sombre and tragic story due to bigotry and social injustice. The dreams of Ammu and Velutha of a future will probably come true, the narrator seems to hint, in the image of the shell rejected by the spider, a shell which is compared to "An antiquated philosophy" (339). So even if the love of Ammu and Velutha is crushed by the caste-system, their legacy is their hope placed in Chappu Thamburam who "fathered future generations." (339)

(b) Paravans on Different Scales

Ironically, through a couple of images, the narrative places the high-caste family on the same level as the Paravan who was murdered for having "entered" a place forbidden to him. Not only does Chacko leave no trace in his daughter Sophie's life as he is replaced by Joe, whom the child considers as her father, but he is also unable to leave a mark on the socio-economic level just as his father was unable to before him. Indeed all his life Pappachi had struggled to be recognised by the English—whom he adulated to the point of not believing his daughter concerning Hollick (42)—in vain. His discovery of the moth is not recognised and he does not receive the expected promotion. Chacko, in his turn, is unable to leave a mark on his community economically as it is not his effort that keeps the factory that his mother created going, but the joint efforts of Ammu and the other two women of the family, Mammachi and Baby Kochamma.

Western education allows Chacko to pompously reflect on his position as brown Sahib without seriously weighing the measure of his words for otherwise he would have been wholly aware of his inadequacy as a "man" in the patriarchal sense. Like his father he is only the outer shell of modernity, displaying outward signs of Western life without the activities that lie behind those outfits; jodhpur pants for the father who never bothered about equitation and Balliol oars for the son who has "slack womanish legs."

Thus in Chacko's own words, the family of Anglophiles is likened to Velutha the Untouchable through the image of erased footprints, "They were a family of Anglophiles. [. . .] and unable to retrace their footsteps because their footprints had been swept away." (52) The same description is given of Velutha, "He left no footprints in sand, no ripples in water, no image in mirrors." (216)

However, Chacko and his community recognise his status, his own sister when critical of his lecherous behaviour with his female employees refers to his "zamindar mentality," whereas in Velutha's case everybody, including his own father Vellya Paapen, cannot see in him more than the Paravan status that his birth gives him. Even Ammu who breaks the barriers to live a relationship with him significantly dreams of him as a one-armed man who does not leave any trace of footsteps. The physical deformity is highly symbolic as it indicates Velutha's lack of agency, due to his birth and therefore his predestined career as a servant of the higher classes. Social determinism is to trace his path in life, and his rebellion ends in death. The lack of an arm and his inability to do more than one thing in Ammu's dream is an echo of her childhood memories when Velutha could only hold out carved objects on his opened palm so that she could pick them up without having to touch his Paravan skin. Significantly, he could only offer, not take. Ammu's descent to his level through sexual intercourse then makes it necessary that she die too, and this is equally foreshadowed in the description of both of them through the image of wood that is burned, "and he shone as though he had been polished with a high-wax body polish" (215) while Ammu had been seeing herself as polished firewood on her wedding photograph. It is logical then that she be later cremated in the same lieu that is consecrated to "beggars, derelicts and the police-custody dead" (162). Velutha having died at the hands of the police while in custody, it is understood that he will be dumped in a pauper's pit or burned in the same crematorium, his father rejects him and would probably not claim his body and his brother is paralysed and unable to act.

Thus in this rigid social system that is Ammu's and Velutha's world, the birth and the geographical location determine the fate of the individual whether s/he be a Dalit or a colonised, leading to the failure of each one's endeavours and dreams, be it recognition by the British, a successful marriage with an Englishwoman or a love affair with a high-caste woman.

2. Religion and the Caste System

(a) Brahmin Jesus versus Untouchable Jesus

There are several images and actions in the novel linking Velutha to the figure of Jesus Christ: through his occupation as a carpenter, his betrayal by one of his group, Comrade Pillai, and the little miracles he achieves. Religion however is denounced throughout the novel as the basis for human savagery and intolerance. So, the reader will discover that the links or comparisons made between Velutha and Jesus are always to Velutha's advantage, perhaps as a means of rehabilitating an individual quasi devoid of the defects that his detractors possess, and yet punished, murdered and registered in official history—police records—as a child kidnapper and a high-caste female's rapist.

In the elaboration of this character, Roy's defence of the Dalits is at its best, most devoted and compassionate to a difficult cause. Velutha is presented as a "God of Small Things" (330). He is the one who creates little marvels out of wood for Ammu as a child and who equally offers her small pleasures as an adult.

> Even later, on the thirteen nights that followed this one, instinctively they stuck to the Small Things [. . .] They had nothing. No future. So they stuck to the small things. (338)

Velutha is described as belonging and ruling over the world of nature, which is separated from the social world on the other side of the river.

> As he rose from the dark river and walked up the stone steps, she saw that the world they stood in was his. That he belonged to it. That it belonged to him. The water. The mud. The trees. The fish. The stars. (333-34)

Velutha can tread on water "He trod water, standing in the middle of the dark river" (333), like Jesus, "And a jewelled Jesus watching. He walked on water. Perhaps." (211) However, Jesus, unlike Velutha and the twins, does not have imagination and creativity, the narrator seems to imply, because he himself is merely a creation, a God of a man-made narrative, at least that is what one might understand from the way religion or at least its use are presented as destructive elements in the protagonists' lives.

> And there it was again. Another religion turned against itself. Another edifice constructed by the human mind, decimated by human nature. (287)

The exceptional quality of Velutha's and the twins' imagination is made clear through the comparison of the children's creative abilities with those of Jesus when they row their boat on land (211) and the dust raised by their activity seems to be an offering made to Jesus (213). This is because Jesus is clearly represented as a mere creation of the mind who is even adapted to the specific local religious norms, a "jewelled Jesus" (211). The author reveals how the religious icon is used by the high castes to suit their needs and is then discarded once they have achieved their goals. Indeed, the calendar which represents Jesus "with lipstick and rouge, and a lurid, jewelled heart . . . Jesus in a mini" (208-9) is something discarded from the Ayemenem house.

Baby Kochamma's bogus religiosity is revealed in her treatment of this materialist representation of Jesus, her use of religion to approach the Irish Father and also in her return for Velutha's deeds, when she leads him to his violent death. Velutha who had "fixed [the garden cherub's] bladder for her" (75), ironically lies dying "in a pool of urine spreading from him" (320), because police violence "resulted in a loss of control over his bladder" (310). There lies the difference between the God of Small Things and Baby Kochamma's Upper Caste God. Through a small detail, the colour red which is on Velutha's "blood-red nails" (307) when he is killed (310-11) and the heart of Jesus who has "lipstick and rouge," yet another link is made and Velutha becomes the symbol of the innocent sacrificed, in his case, to the precepts of Brahmin Christianity, and in Jesus' case for the sake of the redemption of Man.

The reason for this sacrifice is invalid on the religious level for its use is economic and political: this myth and other deep reasons have already been encountered elsewhere: African slaves in southern USA in the past were an economic necessity, the Germans' pretext was being worried about the Jews' "growing presence and power" in their "Aryan" society.

Thus Velutha is linked to Jesus and placed on a higher level giving a very high meaning, almost of sacrifice to happiness—Jesus being the saintly person that he is, and Velutha being almost devoid of defects, and of a far nobler soul than all the high-caste Brahmin characters.

The narrator makes fun of the symbols of the morality of this particular Christianity and its patriarchal order that crushes women. Thus the image of Jesus that Baby Kochamma had in her home, wears a mini and has a lurid heart, "a benign, mouse-haired calendar-Jesus with lipstick and rouge, and a lurid, jewelled heart [. . .] frilled out like a skirt. Jesus in a mini." (208-9)

One must not forget that Velutha is compared to a God, "God of Small Things" (330), and that when he is murdered his toenails are painted red bringing him closer to the figure of Jesus, son of God. Velutha is an untouchable or "Harijan," 'children of God' as Gandhi called them, a name rejected by the community for the name 'Dalit,' 'the Oppressed' thus showing their situation to be a socio-political one, and not a religious one. So, just as Jesus died for man's redemption after being punished for preaching a new religion, Velutha died for preaching and practising equality. Through Rahel's reminiscences, one learns he believed in the right of all layers of society to happiness, but he is to be sacrificed for the maintenance of the social order.

Both Velutha and Jesus as a deity are 'exploited' by people like Mammachi who forgets Velutha's untouchability when she needs something repaired, or like Baby Kochamma who uses religion for her own dark ends, as when she tries to recite the Hail Mary while preparing to go further into criminality to cover her first lies that led to Velutha's bloody death (315). The owner of this gaudy Jesus (208-9) is Baby Kochamma whose use of religion applies double standards to members of the lower and higher castes. Baby Kochamma herself, who is the keeper of religion as it is practised in Ayemenem, as well as the guardian of tradition is represented in a similar manner to the image of Jesus that she chooses, and this description is given again through Rahel's perception, which underlines the loud, garish taste in both descriptions.

> Rahel noticed she was wearing make-up. A sly touch of *rouge* [. . .] her lipstick mouth had shifted slightly off her real mouth. [. . .] She was wearing a lot of *jewellery*. (21-22, my italics)

The guardian of traditions, Baby Kochamma, clings on to ancient beliefs, and the rusted state of her mind is symbolised in the twilight that she lives in with Kochu Maria, through her refusal to use powerful bulbs, "And because the house was locked and dark, and because she only believed in 40-watt bulbs." (21) This petrifaction of time is metaphorically revealed in the unchanged state of her calendar, "Twelve layers of petticoats for the twelve months of the year. None had been torn out." (209) This calendar which Baby Kochamma gives away to the Paravan home (209) also symbolises the status quo of the social hierarchy that Baby Kochamma wants to keep. A status quo in which the members of her caste will continue to generously bestow on the untouchables their unwanted trivia as gifts, and for which the untouchables are to remain thankful forever. This blind gratitude that is sought by the selfish members of the upper castes can be found in the example of Vellya Paapen's "mortgaged eye" (78), an example given by the author to denounce the shameless exploitation of the untouchable as cheap labour even when they are gifted like Velutha (74-77). In this, the calendar is equivalent to the untouchables' school that Baby's father created for the Untouchables (13) and to the untouchable church that the ruling classes had created for the Untouchables, a church which renders explicit the means by which Hindu tradition is preserved through the adaptation of Christianity to the Hindu caste system.

> When the British came to Malabar, a number of Paravans, . . . converted to Christianity and joined the Anglican Church to escape the scourge of Untouchability. [. . .] They were made to have separate churches, with separate services, and separate priests. As a special favour they were even given their own separate Pariah Bishop. (74)

When the policemen cross over to the other side and beat Velutha up with the intention of giving him a good lesson, they murder the imagination and the creativity that he represents. Apart from the little presents that he makes for Ammu and later for her children, Velutha is indeed the only person who is capable of respecting the world of fantasy of the three children.

> It is only now, these years later, that Rahel with adult hindsight, recognised the sweetness of that gesture. A grown man entertaining three racoons, treating them like real ladies. Instinctively colliding in the conspiracy of their fiction, taking care not to decimate it with adult carelessness. Or affection. (190)

Velutha's death occurs only after he is dragged back to the other side by the policemen, and this signifies that he is taken back to the world existing on other side of the river, back to the area where his social and spatial limits are neatly defined. He is dragged away from the a-historical zone where he had crossed into forbidden territory and symbolically entered a space reserved for the upper caste by loving Ammu. The a-historical zone of the lovers' meetings which could have produced another hybrid child, is penetrated by the policemen who change the course of history even before Velutha strays too far as Comrade Pillai takes care to send him to his death.

> His feet walked him to the river. As though they were the leash and he were the dog. History walking the dog. (288)

This image of Velutha being a prisoner of his feet is not surprising as we know that not only Velutha's steps leave no trace, but that when he is sent to a "blind date with history" (282), he is traced and hounded by the policemen. However, they need to drag Velutha back into their own world in order to annihilate him and particularly to make up the proofs of his guilt so that none other would try to transgress the limits that religion and society have imposed. Official history can trace Paravans after all, but it does not allow them to leave their imprint.

(b) Caste-Proof Careers: Manu's Justice

There is a clear parallel between the story of Velutha in the novel and that of Karna in the *Mahabharata*. Karna, abandoned by his mother Kunthi for having been begotten through the Sun-God Surya, while she was a maiden in her father's house, had been raised by commoners. In the same way, Velutha is a child of God, a Harijan, an untouchable abandoned by Mother Earth and whose history is controlled by the ruling castes, the "Brahmin" Christians as compared to the Pandavas. Karna is a nobleman even though he is raised by a charioteer and Velutha is described as far more generous and noble in his spirit than the high-caste people who participate in his death. Velutha, thanks to his talents, is likened to Karna, and like Karna, he will be betrayed by someone close to him. Another religious parallel that can be established is that of Jesus and Judas. Velutha is betrayed by Comrade Pillai in whom he has faith just as Jesus is betrayed by one of his apostles. Moreover, just as Judas is chosen to preach the gospel, Comrade Pillai is one of the local prominent members who advocates that other religion in Kerala, Communism. Judas disclosed Jesus' whereabouts to the chief priests and elders for 30 pieces of silver,[6] equally Comrade Pillai uses the opportunity to his benefit as the following quote reveals.

> To be fair to Comrade Pillai, he did not plan the course of events that followed. He merely slipped his ready fingers into History's waiting glove. It was not entirely his fault that he lived in a society where a man's death could be more *profitable* than his life had ever been. (281, my italics)

Velutha is used to enrich the family, but the day he wages 'war' on them, the Communist Marxist war against the exploitation of the poor by the ruler class, through the demonstration that he participates in, he loses and is slain by the police with the help of Comrade Pillai. Velutha, like Karna, can only serve to a certain point, but cannot reap the product of his hard work, his class war and has to die as Karna in the *Mahabharata*.

Draupadi, one of the strongest female characters in the *Mahabharata*, is the reason for the war between the Pandavas and the Kauravas. Draupadi was humiliated by the Kauravas but her resemblance to Ammu stops at the strong will, for Ammu's wilfulness leads her to give herself to the 'enemy' caste which is not the case of Draupadi. Ammu's love affair with Velutha is considered a humiliation to the family and therefore the police and Baby Kochamma vindicate their lost honour by killing Velutha. Dushasana had indeed tried to strip Draupadi naked in public, and similarly, Velutha has had a love affair with Ammu that has been witnessed by all the villagers. It is Baby Kochamma who sees this affair as a humiliation and has Velutha's blood spilled.

Ammu is not hypocritically revolutionary as the other characters are. Ammu, raised in the Brahmin tradition had received gifts from Velutha as a child without touching him, but when she grows up she no longer allows herself to be contained by what she considers as meaningless traditions. Therefore the reader can understand that she does not consider herself above recognising Velutha publicly even though he is an untouchable, especially as she herself has no Locust Stands I. She is a woman and thus is in a similar position in the factory; like Velutha her hard work goes unrecognised. One might then interpret her reprimanding her children when they call out to Velutha during the demonstration as an attempt to avoid creating trouble in an already troubled situation, or even her fear for him, as he risks being punished for being a threat to the ruler class. It would be meaningful that Ammu tries to protect Velutha at the Communist demonstration because professional promotion or the recognition of the work through equivalent pay is not allowed to untouchables, and we know that she rages against her smug world and hopes it was him the twins had seen (176).

A second interpretation of her reprimanding of her twins would be her dim awareness of her attraction towards Velutha, and her refusal to acknowledge his existence would be a way of trying to shut out her feelings. This fear of recognising her physical attraction to Velutha can be detected in her refusal to use his name. When she is in her room with her children after the nap, she does not use his name and it could be a way of keeping him out of her world. This second interpretation would make their affair seem more logical. Indeed, instead of the affair starting as a device to make the plot move forward—as some could read it so—the affair can be seen as a slow evolution of some obscure and unmanageable feelings of attraction the two would have felt towards each other before they realise they are actually going to have an affair. Having the affair start just the day the family returns from the airport with Sophie Mol, would make it seem rather like a narratorial device that serves the plot and climax of the novel, but taking into account the number of years Ammu was without a husband and also Velutha's constant presence in her sphere, makes the relation plausible, and the possibility that full recognition of the attraction comes on that particular day, triggered off by the scene of Rahel's physical ease with Velutha.

The harvest that Baby Kochamma offers Velutha and the other Dalits is merely a continuation of their repressed condition as a retribution for all the work they do for her caste. Their low-paid hard work is a sign of eternal gratitude to those superior individuals of her class who munificently give the wretched just about enough to survive so as to contain them at the bottommost position of the social ladder where they had long since been from the Vedic times. This unchanged situation exists only for the Untouchables, even though the introduction of Christianity that changed Baby Kochamma's ancestors from Hindu to Christian should have also changed the Dalits' positions.

This leads us to consider sexuality, a major theme, apart from the economic one, through which the status quo of the caste system is upheld.

NOTES

1. Wendy Doniger and K. Brian Smith, trans., *The Laws of Manu* (New Delhi: Penguin, 1991).
2. See Evelyne Hanquart-Turner, "'Never the Twain Shall Meet' de Kipling à Anita Desai, l'union mixte en Inde" for an analysis of the failure of the interracial marriage in postcolonial fiction. Evelyne Hanquart-Turner, ed. *Unions Mixtes et Métissages dans le Monde Anglophone*. Publications du CEREC (Centre d'études et de recherches sur l'empire et le Commonwealth) de l'Université de Paris XII. (Paris: Éditions A3, 1998), pp. 35-65.
3. H.K. Bhabha, *The Location of Culture* (1994; London: Routledge, 1995), p. 16.
4. Daniel Sibony, *Entre-deux l'origine en partage* (Paris: Seuil, 1991). "Quand on découvre avec horreur, effroi ou simple déception—que l'origine, loin d'être pure, est altérée, ça grince, ça

tire sur la corde oedipienne: la mère n'a pas été aussi pure qu'elle l'a fait croire [. . .] D'où les variantes cliniques ou politiques du fanatisme. Le fanatisme, c'est d'avoir à porter en soi un temple *fanum*) où l'on se livre en douce au culte d'une origine impossible à perdre; et par là même supposée pure." pp. 42-43.

5. "When one discovers to one's horror, terror or mere disappointment—that one's origins, far from being pure, are altered, it makes one gnash one's teeth, it strains the Oedipal chord: the mother was not as pure as she had made believe [. . .] which explain the clinical or political variants of fanaticism. Fanaticism is about holding within oneself a temple (fanum) where one discreetly devotes oneself to the cult of an origin that would be impossible to lose: and by that very fact supposedly pure." (My translation).
6. *New Testament and Psalms*. St. Mathew, 26:14-16.

Chapter II

Sexuality

1. Manly Needs

The male characters in the novel are not there to protect the female characters as would be expected in a patriarchal society where the head of the family is the father, husband or brother. The male characters in the novel have more needs, demands and requests than they have things to offer. The female figures are the only ones to be presented as generous with the exception of Velutha.

Male unproductiveness in the novel takes on many aspects amongst which are spiteful destruction of female creativity, clumsy and hopeless endeavours as to construction, and an inability of assuming a paternal role whether it is real or symbolic.[1] The only successful male endeavours that are enumerated are negative and spiteful acts of destruction by petulant and envious male members of the family or the planned crime by the representatives of law in the name of tradition. Pappachi, the twins' grandfather, breaks the bow of his wife's violin and throws it in the river out of sheer jealousy of her creativity and success, refusing to help her in her successful pickling, an activity which he considers as beneath his status of a "high-ranking ex-Government official" (47), although he finds difficulty in adapting to the inactivity of retirement. The fact that she is in her prime while he becomes conscious that he is already an old man only makes matters worse, and explains to some extent the daily beatings she receives. Furthermore, ungrateful for the income provided by her activity, he turns her very success into a fault in order to create the impression that she neglects her wifely duties—which is considered by the community as far more desirable in a wife than leading a successful business—by pretending to sew buttons that are not missing onto his shirts every time visitors are expected in the Ayemenem house. His mean shredding of his daughter's boots as well as his preventing any member of the family to sit in the Plymouth he bought from an old Englishman are examples that shed more light on his immature and spiteful character and his inability to accept assertiveness in the women of his family or to allow them any measure of pleasure out of utter resentment.

Equally barren are his son Chacko's actions. From the miniature planes that he never succeeds to construct correctly in order to make them fly, to the innovations he makes to run the factory as a learned man, all his enterprises are hopeless, luckless and vowed to failure. The machines that he buys for labelling the pickle bottles, cost way too much for the family, and slowly but surely, Chacko starts the slide to bankruptcy after his mother had spent years building up the factory from a mere stall. He mortgages the family's rice-fields to obtain bank loans that finance his extravagant "Pickle Baron dreams" (57). When he installs the advertising board on the car, Chacko only manages to achieve ridicule, and earns an embarrassed comment from his ex-wife whom he venerates. Ultimately, male actions are exposed as a failure as in the emblematic disintegration of the moths into dust (155), the pins that had served to visibly secure Pappachi's discovery, only pinpointing the resulting futility and emptiness of the male's highest ambitions.

Concerning their roles in the family, the male characters either reject fatherhood or are unable to play their roles as fathers due to their weakness and preference to being mothered. When they play any role at all, it is only the darker aspects linked to these social masks that are revealed. Pappachi is feared by his daughter Ammu for the random beatings she occasionally gets along with her mother, and Chacko has to resort to violence to preserve his mother. Chacko, inheriting some of his father's characteristics, is revealed to be unreliable, for Margaret Kochamma soon realises that he is unable to work or take care of himself, let alone of a family. She divorces him when Sophie is born, so as not to be a mother to her husband as well as to her newborn baby. Even as a surrogate father figure Chacko fails, for he is unable to recognise his niece Rahel's need for his love when she indirectly questions him on her position once his own daughter, Sophie, will be there (118).

In fact, Chacko's lack of feelings goes further, he actually finds it hilarious to point out both to Ammu and to the twins that Ammu is moneyless and therefore powerless, "Chacko told Rahel and Estha that Ammu had no Locusts Stand I [. . .] of his size and fatness" (57). Indeed, Chacko taunts his sister Ammu with "What's yours is mine and what's mine is also mine" (57)—despite the fact that she is the one who is running it with Velutha and the two older women of the family, also reveals him as insensitive to the twins. The twins, who do not wholly understand their Uncle Chacko's bickering with their mother over the rights to the factory—despite the fact that he owns it as Kerala's inheritance laws privilege the son over the daughter—still turn to him constantly for paternal love. Finally, they have to accept him as an individual "Chacko" instead of begging for his love in public.

> Rahel and Estha couldn't call him Chachen [father] because when they did, he called them Chetan [older brother] and Cheduthi [older brother's wife]. If they called him Uncle he called them Aunty, which was embarrassing in Public. So they called him Chacko. (37)

Male characters do not seem to give their offspring any positive elements, as revealed in Ammu's perception of the twins' 'monstrous' inheritance from their Baba, as their eyes are half-open in their sleep. Ammu who avoids talking of their father and refuses any influence from that quarter readily recognises in them only the following negative inheritance.

> Her twins were sleeping the way they did when they were exhausted—with their eyes half open, two small monsters. That they got from their father. (331)

Likewise Rahel recognises her grandfather's cruelty in her own mother who has inherited this cruel streak and capacity for revealing sudden bouts of temper or anger, a cruelty symbolised by the moth.

> "In the years to come, . . . and his children's children." (49), "Rahel saw that Ammu . . . that her eyes had become hard, like marbles. Like Pappachi's in the Vienna studio photograph. How Pappachi's moth whispered in his children's veins!" (72)

Thus Rahel's reminiscences tell the reader that women nurture and mother the male and create viable projects, whereas the male characters father only degeneracy, sterility and destruction.

2. Sexless Widows and Divorcees

(a) Castrating Mothers

Divorced and widowed women instantly cease to have a sexual life—at least visibly—along with the change of their legal status or the death of their husband. However, the sexual energy that cannot be purged even if suppressed or controlled can turn into energy used elsewhere, or it can also "turn" in the sense of becoming altered in a negative manner.

Mammachi's sexuality turns into a perverse and active interest in her son's sex life that transforms itself into a symbolic castration of the son as with the goddess Kali who accepts testicles as food.[2] Sudhir Kakar[3] explains this as a self-castration by the son in an unconscious attempt to defend his sexuality against his mother's overwhelming sexuality which is represented in the myth of Shiva and Devi. Devi, the Mother Goddess, one of whose avatars is the terrible anthropophagous Kali, brings an army of goddesses out of her mouth in order to defeat Ruru's army. She then informs Shiva that now that she has helped him combat the monster, her army would eat him as a means of compensation. Mothers' games with their babies sometimes include the pretence of 'eating' them up. Shiva pretends to accept but informs her that he is impure and therefore unfit for consumption. He then proposes his testicles:

> I will give you something never tasted by anyone else: the two balls resembling fruits below my navel. Eat the testicles that hang there and be satisfied.[4]

Mammachi, the reader is told, once rescued by her son from her daily beatings at the hand of her husband, takes "her wifely luggage" and commits it to Chacko's care (168). Her son then becomes "Her Man. Her only Love" (168). Pappachi never sets his hand on her again and the reader can perhaps rightly include sexual intercourse as well. Still, Mammachi can live her sexuality by proxy through the control she exerts over her son's sexuality, which she runs according to feudally financial rules. Significantly, she is the actual 'Modalali' (122), or landlord, whom everyone turns to in times of crisis or decision-making concerning the running of the factory thus depriving Chacko of his 'manliness' or male role.

Mammachi's erasure of her son's maleness comes through the form of her 'consumption' of his virility as she takes over the control of his sex life in a subliminal replacement of her lost sexuality with her husband who no longer even addresses her. In fact, her very devotion to her son divests him of his feudal power over his female employees as his various employees receive money from his mother to feed their families. In this manner, Chacko, probably aware of the fact that the only reason his female employees succumb to his sexual demands is that he is their employer, is denied this last power by his mother who in reality is the true landlord. In addition to her position as Modalali, she secretly pays them for the sexual favours her son obtains from them, even though she maintains her son's high illusions of landlordism.

Through the sums of money paid by Mammachi in order to separate "Needs from Feelings," (169) she also keeps intact her son's feelings of which she wishes to be the sole beneficiary. Even the love that Chacko still feels for Margaret Kochamma is obscured in Mammachi's imagination as she represents to herself their hypothetical relation as a vulgar commerce in which Margaret Kochamma receives money in exchange for sex from her former husband. All this happens through a strange transaction in which an unknowing Margaret Kochamma is supposed to have accepted the money that Mammachi places daily in her dirty linen. The money is in fact is collected by the laundry woman. Unaware of all this hocus pocus going on behind her back, Margaret Kochamma becomes a prostitute paid by Mammachi just like the female factory workers as Mammachi is jealous of her son's love for his former wife, "the undercurrent of sexual jealousy that emanated from Mammachi" (329).

Mammachi, while providing every necessary space for her son's sexual needs, strips him of the very sexual power that he imposes on his female employees, for, like a shadow pimp, she turns Chacko's apartments into a kind of brothel by building a separate entrance to it, her prim toleration of his manly needs being the price to pay to keep him home. Her going to the extent of slipping money into an unknowing Margaret Kochamma's clothes in the laundry basket is a symbolic act of possession of her son's sexuality. In her twisted logic if every woman is paid, then intercourse with them becomes a pure physical reaction like a virgin adolescent polluting his bed sheets but still not bringing in a female rival to his first love, his mother. Mammachi can therefore live her pure love with the son who has become the only man of her life, as is revealed by the narrator's underlining of an incestuous undercurrent in her motherly feelings, "She was aware of his libertine relationships with the women in the factory, but *had ceased to be hurt* by them" (168, my italics). Thus, Chacko's feelings, if they are separated from needs by his mother's strange transactions of which the real motives are known only to herself, are left to his mother.

Baby Kochamma is not a mother figure but her contribution to erasing the male is the most violent. It is primarily through her intervention that Velutha is literally castrated by the police who crush his genitals with their boots. The meaning of Baby Kochamma's act can be inscribed in the female competition for male interest in a patriarchal society and approval.

> Under male supremacy women's status depends greatly on male approval. If we don't conform we pay heavy penalties. It means that many women mutilate and injure themselves, [. . .] This is important in the maintenance of male power. It prevents us seeing each other as allies, but sets us up as enemies, always in competition.[5]

Baby Kochamma feels spite on witnessing Ammu dare to snatch a second instance of carnal pleasure through the affair she has with an untouchable while she herself had given up her womanhood or sexuality. Her jealousy and prejudice lead her to 'prefer' an "Irish Jesuit smell," comments the narrator. Baby Kochamma stands for the symbolic mother, who having been deprived of sexuality in order to achieve recognition in society, in her turn deprives her daughter of sexual contentment in the war for recognition in the eyes of the male. In fact, Baby Kochamma's adolescent wish that is limited to be "Close enough to smell his [Father Mulligan's] beard" (24) is only a perverse conversion of her suppressed sexuality. She uses—just as Father Mulligan himself does—religion as a means of replacing physical love. Her questions on religion are the only means to keep him close to her so that she can enjoy the physical presence and speech of the monk as a surrogate for sex (24).

Baby's sexual jealousy that lead her to the extent of her destroying her niece and to indirectly causing Velutha's castration and death by the police officers, just as Mammachi's feeling sick at her own mental representation of her daughter having sex with an untouchable, are the result of the conditioning which reduces women's minds to conform to the image of the pure-minded sexless widow or female in general.

Both women have in mind an ideal of the marriageable, loveable male: a high-caste Brahmin regardless of his qualities as a husband for Mammachi and a casteless member of the conqueror race for Baby Kochamma. Moreover, the women themselves cannot see themselves under a different image, their idea of what they should appear like and how they should behave being instilled into them from their early childhood. This leads a large Baby Kochamma to manifest what we could call Cinderella Syndrome symptoms when she exposes her tiny feet for the visitors to marvel at what she believes is their daintiness, forgetting that the contrast with her big body might make her appear ungainly.

> The controlling effects of the male gaze are, of course, apparent in other areas besides personal relationships. [. . .] It simultaneously enables men to cope with the threat which femininity represents, allowing them, as Laura Mulvey suggests, to distance the image of woman, fetishizing her and regarding her voyeuristically as a 'spectacle.' Women certainly do achieve a degree of narcissistic pleasure from their position as focus of the 'Look.' However, they pay a heavy price for it in terms of coercion and control.[6]

This need to conform to a ready-made model of femininity is what leads Baby Kochamma to pay the price of a life of loneliness as she waits for Father Mulligan her whole life until she hears of his death. Once Father Mulligan is dead, Baby Kochamma strips him of his saffron robes in her mind, in order to return him to the image of the prince charming that she desired as an adolescent girl many years ago. Baby Kochamma, neither widow, nor divorcee sublimates her frustrated virginity into garden-designing, labouring in the heat of the afternoons to grow exotic plants and daily adding the same entry into her diary so as to keep romance in her life. Having given up her own casteless lover, though he is of a 'superior' kind, as he belongs to the ruling 'race,' her adolescent wish to "smell" Father Mulligan's beard, is opposed to her shuddering at the Paravan smell that her niece has tolerated. The narrator slyly underlines her preference for an Irish-Jesuit smell thus hinting at the sexual jealousy that motivates Baby's actions when the tragedy is set into motion by her.

Ammu is not faultless either as her frustration at not being able to live her love life or rather, her desperation at being forced to conform to a single role, that of sexless motherhood, turns into a violent rejection of her twins as burdens in a moment of desperation due to her situation. This indirectly leads to the tragic events that build up crescendo to Estha's consecutive alienation. By unconsciously depriving her twins of a surname and a social status through her hesitation between her husband's name and her father's name, she also divests Estha of the possibility of giving his own version of the story. Indeed 'Estha Unknown' cannot give his version of the story. The unconscious matriarchal struggle for social position and for power in Ammu's conscious hesitation between the choice of two names that she did not consider as a real choice for a woman, turns into a symbolic war of origins with dire consequences on the innocent children who become rootless. This reminds us of Kerala's matrilineal past, unfathomable to the Victorian mind and thus deemed immoral, so polyandry and matrilineal inheritance were erased and replaced by the Western Christian model. The terrible consequences on Estha's position later on in the police station can be seen as an echo of the situation of young Malayalee males in the early

1960s due to the changes brought by the British in the Victorian period through the Nair Regulation laws. The sociologist Irawati Karve's survey[7] had found that the young men in Kerala thought of their fathers as male concubines to their mothers.[8] A strong female, more so one that controls property is a 'non-traditional' image and the British intervention changed the laws concerning polyandry and land possession, therefore the perception of the female in Kerala.

The male fear of the female is alluded to by the narrator as being amongst the major reasons for society's resorting to violence to uphold its laws.

> Feelings of contempt, born of inchoate, unacknowledged fear—civilisation's fear of nature, men's fear of women, power's fear of powerlessness. (308)

This is particularly true in the case of the sexually potent female figure as in the female divinity, Kali. Wendy Doniger stresses the sexual aspect related to the male fear of the female in the Hindu psyche.

> The dominant woman is dangerous in Hindu mythology, and the dominant goddess expresses this danger in several but closely related ways. She appears as the killer of her demon lover, beheading him in a symbolic castration; she dances on the corpse of her consort, impaling herself upon his still inanimate phallus.[9]

Both mothers, Mammachi and Ammu, are castrating figures each in her own way. Mammachi appropriates her son's sexuality and Ammu castrates her husband as a father figure and therefore her son. Indeed, Ammu symbolically deprives the first of a space in her children's lives through her refusal of their reproducing their father's behaviour, though he had in fact already relinquished his role as a father. Estha is not allowed to "shiver his leg" as his father did thus Ammu erases any mimicry that the son undertakes to resemble his father regardless of the fact that the action quoted was not worth imitating. She then deprives the second of space in society through her erasure of his surname and its indirect consequences, "Estha occupied very little space in the world" (11).

Baby Kochamma and Mammachi have both in a sense replaced sexual enjoyment with a desire for control, one tries to tame wild or exotic plants, land and the weather through a rigid discipline for years and the other through the control she exerts over her son's love life (26-27). In both cases, this surrogate activity is tinted with bitterness and its fuelling factor is a mingling of sentiments totally opposing the original ones, like sharing or love, such as jealousy, hatred, envy. Jealousy, hatred, envy are the feelings that drive Baby Kochamma forward; jealousy of the twins' carefree attitude which in her view does not befit their inferior fatherless position and jealousy of Ammu's sauciness and later love affair with the untouchable worker, Velutha. Mammachi's fuel is jealousy and possessiveness.

The instances of Mammachi and Baby Kochamma's condemnation of Ammu's affair with Velutha are not solely linked to a question of caste and religion. Before this, Ammu had returned to her parents' home un-welcomed, for a divorced woman is ostracized by the other members of society and mostly by the women. This need to see the other go uncomplainingly through all kinds of bad treatments from the male is an illustration of the lack of solidarity amongst women. The first is the competition provoked by male supremacy in a patriarchal society and that was evoked earlier, and the second is the need to have fellow-sufferers for company as well as the resentment resulting from seeing others fight against a fate that one has accepted as one's natural destiny.

Female activity consists of nurturing the ungrateful male and in sowing the seeds of their own continued repressed condition. Mothering the male then also consists of crushing those female wills that oppose male dominance.

So as a conclusion one can say that man-less women in India are not without desire and resort to the liberation of their sexual energy through other means, mostly creativity and power. However the result is devastating for the male castrated either psychologically like Chacko, mentally like Estha or finally, physically like Velutha.

(b) Elderly Virgins

Miss Mitten and Baby Kochamma reflect the stereotype of the joyless and bitter spinster. Miss Mitten is unable to adapt her thinking to the twins but can only impose rigid way of teaching while Baby classifies her interactions with people as things she did for people and things they did not do for her.

Baby Kochamma wears lipstick and jewels in a last attempt to live what she had lost as a young girl. The image that she wishes to project is still that which she had wanted to conform to as a young girl in the colonial time. For, as an adolescent she converted to the religion of the young Irish monk in order to be integrated to his world, and as an old lady she still adheres to the item which dispenses the 'first world's' ways; no longer morality and civilisation through the Bible, but beauty and 'first world panache' through Satellite Television. Indeed, if Shakespeare is her reference while it is Kathakali for the twins, the television is the only means of living for this elder woman, who has shut her own world out, opening the window only to "Take a Breath of Fresh Air." Everything that she does, even her fears of being robbed, is in relation to thc news she watches on her television. Her hair is cut in a bob and she wears lipstick most probably due to the influence of the serials that she watches on her television. Indeed, Baby lives by proxy the lives of the blondes with "smart repartees" as she remembers and savours them during the following day. The narration in fact espouses her struggle against fate as it moves backwards to the days when she had been desirable to the missionary.

On the whole, both Baby and Miss Mitten represent the negative female figure that is ruled by Thanatos as opposed to the figure of Ammu, ruled by Eros and who represents the joy of living despite her harsh circumstances, "She danced for him. [. . .] She lived." (337) Indeed, Baby Kochamma plots and leads to the death of Velutha who brought love to Ammu, and Miss Mitten sees only dark, death-related things in others, such as the 'Satan' she professes to see in the twins' eyes.

Baby Kochamma is often represented in a setting of physical and mental imprisonment. First, she is seen in closed, confined quarters such as the monastery and later the closed Ayemenem home; the only time she is represented in the open air is when she is in love and that is pushed back in the past, a lost opportunity that makes her bitter and sadistic in her behaviour with the twins and their mother. On the opposite, Ammu and Velutha meet in nature and are in communion with the most positive aspects of it while sharing their love, "On that boat-shaped piece of earth." (337)

This former aspiring nun, and one must remind that it was for purely sexual and emotional motives for a man and not for religious reasons, is described in opposition to the nuns of the film the children watch, thus underlining the lack of spirituality in her. The author gives her an unsophisticated physical appearance, for her breasts are described as "melons" in addition to negative traits like excess body weight and bad breath as we can infer from these lines.

> Rahel studied her baby grand aunt's enormous legs. [. . .] Fat knees dimpled. Hair on them. [. . .] Bosom swinging low. Melons in a blouse. (95)
>
> Quiet nuns . . . gathered like ants around a crumb of toast. [. . .] No hair on their knees. No melons in their blouses. And their breath like peppermint. (99)

This image of ants around a piece of toast is not without reminding us of the image of the sea of eggs around a yolk, which other similarly religious congregation leaves Baby Kochamma out of it, thus ironically depriving her of Father Mulligan. In fact, in her hypocritical conversion to Catholicism, was a vain attempt to get closer to the man she loved. As for Father Mulligan, he later converts to Hinduism. Baby Kochamma is thus deprived of womanhood and religious sisterhood, turning her into an enormous, frustrated, embittered old virgin baby grandaunt.

3. Forbidden Territory

The greatest taboo in all societies remains incest; some of its forms are more condemnable than others because of the closeness of the blood relationship and the religious and moral implications behind that particular relationship. Literature has examples of these transgressions and the misery and tragedy they lead to, the most known example being the story of Oedipus. However, when Roy inserts an incestuous relationship between Estha and Rahel, it is important to underline, that a tragedy has already taken place in their lives and this incestuous union remains unknown and unpunished. In addition, the initial sexual relation which leads to the tragedy is much less condemnable than the twins' incestuous union. What is the role of this physical union of the twins, which is rendered in a very different manner than the union of Ammu and Estha? Most important, when considering reader-response, the incestuous union did not provoke the fury of the plaintiff who sued Roy for the logically acceptable love-making scene between Velutha and Ammu.

The questions one should ask oneself are: What is the weight of a revealed incest in a traditional society compared to other socially unacceptable relations? What does the incest stand for in the novel? Pramod K. Nayar reads it most obviously as a subversion and also as a deprivation of the concerned of their significance through the image of emptiness and silence fitting like "stacked spoons."[10]

It is notable that an incestuous union, unless when revealed to the eyes of justice as a rape, is considered more in terms of morality and the involved person's sanity than as a crime. The law applicable to incest is more so the religious one, which is far more important in the human psyche than the man-made laws. Thus if a disapproved sexual relation takes place, the worst that can happen is temporary punishment, or ostracism. Nevertheless, when it is the case of incest, it is the whole order of things in the world that is upset, thus casting its actors out of any human society. In the novel however, Ammu's affair with Velutha takes on a disproportionate size in the minds of a religious community which has incorporated ancient Hindu laws and practices into an imported Christianity. The outcome of Ammu's relation is death, not even banishment. The twins being psychologically affected by their community's treatment of themselves, and to a certain extent, socially dead to their Syrian Christian community in Kerala, their violation of the code can only be greater than that of their mother so as to justify their ostracism. The twins had already been cast out of their society because of their being an issue from a disapproved intercommunity and interfaith marriage, so they already know the dire circumstance of ostracism. Therefore, on the one hand, their union can be interpreted not only as an act of defiance in order to avenge Ammu's death and confirm her rebellion or to replace her act on a lower scale of reprehensibility by placing themselves on a further level of condemnation. On the other hand, this act also finally symbolically places them on the side of the rejected, the marginalized, for all that the twins had lived as victims, was never due to any action that they had chosen to commit and which was against the rules. Therefore only by committing the incest can they "deserve" the void in which they have erred since Velutha's murder. They have nothing left to lose:

> And for the little family curled up and asleep on a blue cross-stitch counterpane? What came for them?
>
> Not death. Just the end of living. (321)

It is therefore no small coincidence that their act of incest is placed in proximity to the part of the narrative where the reader discovers Ammu's intention of joining Velutha.

But the author's description of the incest reveals in truth a far more humane object than a simple defiance and transgression of the various laws that had led to the disruption of their childhood. In fact the act is the logical conclusion of the twins' rejoining after years of separation. The incest cannot be seen as a sexual act as the twins are described as one person. Indeed, "Esthappen and Rahel thought of themselves together as Me, and separately, individually, as We or Us." (2) Furthermore, the description of their bodies during the incest with a now familiar phrase to the reader "like stacked spoons" (328), fits their complementary natures and features and sends us back to their symbiosis, "That the emptiness in one twin was only a *version* of the quietness in the other. That the two things fitted together. Like stacked spoons. Like familiar lovers' bodies." (20, my italics) The non-sexual nature of the union is underlined as the narrator repeatedly compares the twins to a rare breed that has one identity, and elsewhere even to one single physical entity, "Rahel never wrote to him. There are things that you can't do—like writing letters *to a part of yourself.* To your feet or hair. Or heart." (164, my italics)

Despite the obvious allusion to the various characters' crossing forbidden territory, the limit that the twins transgress can apply to others in society but it does not wholly apply to them. This incestuous union then is the expression of the strength of the bonds of siblings, and according to reader-response theory, the reader who is shocked by their act is then applying his or her negative perception of their act to their pure feelings. The act is the expression of Rahel's compassion for her alienated brother and an attempt to shake him out of his world of self-inflicted punishment. Judas' conscience rightly torments him for having in effect betrayed Jesus, whereas Estha wrongly torments his soul and mind for Velutha's death, taking on the burden of Baby Kochamma's scheming because of one word he had uttered under pressure.

> The word Estha's octopus couldn't get at: Yes. Hovering didn't seem to help. It was lodged there, deep inside some fold or furrow, like a mango hair between the molars. That couldn't be worried loose. (32)

The incest is Rahel's tentative to reunite with her long-lost dizygotic twin, after having been violently separated from him: "On the station platform Rahel doubled over and screamed and screamed" (326). It is also Estha's attempt to retrieve his lost mother whose very funeral he was deprived of:

> Twenty-three years later, Rahel, dark woman in a yellow T-shirt, turns to Estha in the dark.
>
> 'Esthapappychachen Kuttappen Peter Mon,' she says.
>
> She whispers.
>
> She moves her mouth.
>
> Their beautiful mother's mouth.
>
> Estha, sitting very straight, waiting to be arrested, takes his fingers to it. To touch the words it makes. To keep the whisper. (327)

Obviously, on a first reading, the act then becomes doubly reprehensible, as Estha searches for signs of his mother in his sister. However, compared to the attitude of their grandmother towards her son Chacko, the relation is presented as healing for Estha can finally express his grief. On the contrary, Mammachi's undercurrent of sexual jealousy towards her former daughter-in-law and her complicated arrangements to pass Margaret off as a whore in her mind are clearly unhealthy (168-69).

Repression of her sexuality is the only means for the female to keep a place in society, the contrary leading to the worst fate. The very description of Ammu's walk, which later leads her to walk fast, then run to her first rendezvous with Velutha, reveals the weight of the moral laws that define up to the manner in which a woman moves her body, "As though she had temporarily set aside the morality of motherhood and divorceehood. Even her walk changed from *a safe mother-walk* to another wilder sort of walk." (44, my italics) This verifies the society's fears of woman's physical desires which had been reflected in the novels of male authors a century earlier, and one can say with reason that it is applicable at the end of the twentieth century.

> They [the authors] saw a woman's sexuality as a dangerous disruptive force which had to be controlled and channelised, while maternity was necessary for the service and nurturing of the community and so was venerated and lauded. Being made to renounce her sexuality the widow is first enclosed and then elevated to a superhuman level where she is no longer subject to the pains and pleasures of ordinary human existence but is transformed into a benign sustaining archetypal mother.[11]

Ammu, who had followed her instinct in living, tracing her own path out of the socially approved one, will die alone in a cheap lodge with no one to come to her help as she suffocates to death because of her asthma. Not only the death in utter loneliness, but also the narrator's dark-humoured comments on the aspect of Ammu's eye, "She had a deep blue sac under one eye that was bloated like a bubble. As though her eye had tried to do what her lungs couldn't" (162), links her death to the death of a sparrow which had entered *a place* not meant for it. "A sparrow lay dead on the back seat. [. . .] She died on the back seat, with her legs in the air. Like a joke." (296)

In fact, the language of the novel which espouses the point of view of the seven-year-old twins seems to take up their view of death when Ammu's death is evoked. The event seen through their apprehending of the world through a combination of the mastery of language and playing with it as the twins are made to look up words every time a difficult word or a concept appears.

> . . . and they are as old as Ammu when she died. Thirty one.
> Not old.
> Not young.
> But a viable die-able age. (5)

Ammu's death is more than fate playing a nasty joke on her. It is the direct result of her having crossed the limits imposed by her community. Her act is the negation of generations of her family's conforming to the rules imposed to live in an organised group, thus threatening her family with marginalisation as Mammachi's thoughts, exposed by the omniscient narrator, reveal:

> She had defiled generation of breeding . . . and brought the family to its knees. . . . They'd nudge and whisper. It was all finished now. Mammachi lost control. (258)

When the female replaces the male guardian, and is faced with an unauthorised act, she loses her capacity to act for the very reason that she is in territory that is out of her scope; therefore she loses control over a situation which she is not used to facing due to her own habit of being guarded, confined, to a limited sphere. Mammachi's loss of control and her unleashed fury will set the actions in motion so that neither Ammu nor Velutha can escape the consequences of their act. The understanding between Baby and Mammachi to have Velutha and Ammu punished stems from their own inability to act in the face of a situation that goes beyond their field of competence, as both women have accepted the constraints of their gender. Thus female solidarity between Ammu and those who have followed the rules becomes impossible as she no longer shares their values and their victimhood of pious, suffering Sitas. Her very individuality in her research for life and its pleasures antagonises these women.

The final issue then is casting her out for she had crossed the limits imposed on her social role as an asexual mother, as is revealed in the sexuality implied in this description of Ammu where there is a change in her from a "safe mother-walk to another *wilder sort of walk*" (44, my italics). The word 'wildness' here indicates her untamed sexuality that will express itself outside the sanctified relationship of marriage with a man of the same social background.

NOTES

1. This paragraph and others in the book have already been published in a paper entitled "(M)Othering the Male in *The God of Small Things*," *Arundhati Roy: The God of Small Things. L'hybridité célébrée* (Gallix, François. Mallard Editions. Collection Angloscopies, 2002).
2. Kali, Devi Mata or Durga are various avatars of the strongest of the female divinities in the Hindu pantheon.
3. Sudhir Kakar, *Moksha. The Inner World. A Psychoanalytic Study of Childhood and Society in India* (1978; New Delhi: Oxford India, 2002).
4. *Padma Purana*, 5. 26, qtd. Sudhir Kakar, p. 98.
5. Rhodes Dusty and McNeill Sandra, ed., *Women against Violence against Women* (Onlywomen Press, 1985), p. 255, qtd. Paulina Palmer, *Contemporary Women's Fiction: Narrative Practice and Feminist Theory* (Hertfordshire: Harvester Wheatsheaf, 1989), p. 33.
6. Paulina Palmer, p. 34.
7. Irawati Karve, *Kinship Organisation in India* (Bombay: Asia, 1953), pp. 297-99. Qtd. Susie Tharu and K. Lalitha, *Women Writing in India: 600 B.C. to the Present* (Delhi: Oxford University Press, 1995), Vol. I, p. 159.
8. Cf. Section 'Matriarchal Kerala' in chapter one.
9. Wendy Doniger O'Flaherty, *Women, Androgynes and Other Mythical Beasts* (London, Chicago: University of Chicago Press, 1980), p. 77.

10. Pramod K. Nayar, "Troping Silence: Oversignification and Liminality in *The God of Small Things*," in R.K. Dhawan.
11. Rajul Sogani, *The Widow in Nineteenth Century Indian Novels (1857-1907)*, unpublished M.Phil. Dissertation, 1990, Delhi University, p. 61. Qtd. S.K. Das, *A History of Indian Literature. 1911-1956. Struggle for Freedom; Triumph and Tragedy* (New Delhi: Sahitya Akademi, 1995), p. 336.

Chapter III

Palimpsest

Arundhati Roy's 'play' with words does not aim at the celebration of English for the sake of the language itself, nor does it promote an Indian use of the English language while keeping in mind the huge Anglophone market. The novel rather creates an idiom to convey the deepest meanings behind the simplest words used by children. The feat of the author resides in her ability to enter a child's mind, or should one say retain the child's vision, its capacity of creation, and wonder, and expose its reasoning in order to interpret and relate the happenings in an adult world. The power of this novel does not really reside in its subject matter, for human lives have been through the same tragic experiences since time immemorial, but in the linguistic and technical skill with which this universal experience is related rendering it a unique narrative. Roy has created a language that reflects the world as it is perceived by two seven-year old twins.

The extraordinary use of the English language conveys with accuracy the world as it is experienced by children. Indeed the smallest details that matter to a child are translated with an utmost care. Words do confer importance and dignity to the smallest of emotions as no single event is considered trivial. By the end of the novel, the reader realises that even the smallest of pleasures, even the ones dreamt can contribute to a fragile happiness. The narrator uses the children's words in the narrative even if it is given mainly through the eyes of an adult Rahel.

Voicing children's feelings through adult's words implies the risk of substituting their unique experience with a social comment or diluting their pain and joy through the summarising of precise moments that need to be brought back in their entirety. Roy has managed to convey the tragic while keeping a seven-year-old child's perception free from adult colouring.

Roy's is a powerful narrative of an age-old theme, love, told in a singularly creative and poetic prose told by an omniscient narrator and focalising mostly on the point of view of Rahel, one of the main characters; these narratives mingle with others.[1] The novel is a blend of autobiographical elements and of fiction which springs from the school of experience while the layers of narrative seem to come from the school of architecture. The main action of the story is the accidental drowning of Rahel's half-English cousin, Sophie Mol during her visit to Kerala, which triggers a series of tragic events but there are layers of tales to be lifted to uncover the whole of the tragedy. The plot is contained in the period of a bit more than a fortnight and yet it takes twenty three years and a new narration of that past time as well as a hint of the narratives of ancient times for the missing parts to be added to the story when it is narrated once again through a different voice and point of view. The main drama, which is the brutal murder of Velutha, the beloved untouchable friend of Rahel and her twin brother Estha, which they witness in silent horror, shatters their lives as well as their mother, Ammu's life. Rahel, dizygotic twin sister of the now silent Estha, summons their joint memories to relate their stories as well as their dead mother's, twenty-three years after the 'stories' given by their great-aunt, Baby Kochamma, and the police, who were instrumental in disrupting their lives. To be deciphered, this palimpsest is to be traced through memory, time and voice.

1. Writing and Re-Membering

The novel begins with a caveat in the form of an epigraph from novelist, literary critic and essayist, John Berger: "Never again will a single story be told as though it is the only one," clearly indicating to the reader to pay heed to the peripheral stories that accompany the main one, and to read the subtexts underlying the official narratives. This caution also serves to claim the reader's sympathy from the beginning, particularly, if one considers the negative manner in which a love story between a high-caste divorcee and an untouchable worker is likely to be received in a caste-ridden society, notwithstanding governmental efforts to help untouchables gain access to education and work, the spheres they are normally kept locked out of.

The narrative is a palimpsestic one which re-members the shattered histories of Rahel's brother's and mother's lives by inscribing on the known version of the tragedy, as recounted by her great-aunt, Baby Kochamma, the silenced truth some twenty-three years later. The narrative simultaneously comments on the values upheld by society, through the maintenance of religious laws and social rules of interaction as opposed to the twins' innocent world. The narrator brands the Keralite or Indian society's age-old un-fair/y tales of decency, respectability, justice or generosity, colouring the events that are narrated with the scathing comments of an adult Rahel on the degeneration of values. The narrator's hindsight is associated with a major focalisation on the perception of the two helpless twins in the re-narration of the tragic events while filling in the gaps of understanding that had served to utterly ruin Rahel's family when she and her brother were led to believe that they were saving their mother by denouncing their beloved untouchable friend, Velutha.

This child-dominated narrative is a postmodernist tale of what lies beneath mainstream myths of propriety, family ties or the inherent decency of members of the high caste. Behind the veneer of idealised, genteel "Touchable" communities, the reader discovers people who resemble wicked witches (Baby Kochamma) and gnomes (Kochu Maria) who do not guard underground treasures but tradition, and who crowd in on innocent childhood to delimit the borders of the printable version of a criminal story, turned into a "History lesson" and that the narrator revisits like a detective unearthing hidden facts.

Using some of the elements and vocabulary of the fairy tale, in the various allusions to the fairy and folk tales that constitute the child's world, the narrator presents us with the real life version of an un-fair/y tale, where a wicked witch disguised as a fairy godmother tricks two unknowing children out of their childhood and into tragedy. Baby Kochamma, "like a fairy godmother presented them with a solution" (317). This 'solution' actually leads their mother out of her happy, fairy-tale dream world (332), to sorrow in real life. Indeed, if one considers the structure of the fairy tale, the novel has almost all the ingredients. Ammu is the beautiful princess whose heart can be won by a brave or intelligent subject from her father's Kingdom. However in a caste-ridden society, the fairy tale turns sour. Ammu is truly the beautiful high-caste grand-daughter of the local Lord, Reverend E. John Ipe and his wife (Ammachi) who has built the school for Untouchables where Velutha is later to be educated. Velutha is the humble citizen whose practical intelligence saves the Kingdom, here Paradise Pickles and Preserves, to which he is invaluable, unlike Ammu's brother, Chacko, the official owner who does own this to Comrade Pillai, "He's invaluable. He practically runs the factory" (279). But Velutha's participation can only be grudgingly recognised, as he is an untouchable. He therefore cannot win Ammu's hand and live happily ever after with her, just as his work is paid less and his status cannot be made official.

(a) Hindsight and Understanding

Only later do the twins understand their mother's role in the family's tragedy and Rahel symbolically revives her mother's defiance of the Love Laws by committing an incestuous act at the same age as her mother was when she died. Before this, she summons her memories, as well as her twin brother's—as the narrator underlines their having "joint identities," to relate the first sexual transgression and thus give meaning to this second sexual transgression of the Love Laws.

Through the image of the bracelet that Rahel is offered by her mother, with serpent heads—symbolising sexuality—she passes on to her daughter her rebellious position. Indeed, the 'illicit' relation that Ammu has is reflected in the manner in which both women consider the male with whom they will have what should be called 'physical intercourse' though the act by Rahel has a far deeper meaning. Just as Ammu watches Velutha as if he were her child, "and she smiled down at him as though he was her child" (336), Rahel watches Estha, "with the curiosity of a mother watching her wet child" (93). The incestuous relation or the transgression of the Love Laws is already predicted here.

Rahel has come back from the United States to put order into their lives. The reader is given the whole story in the first chapter with the omission of the details that had—due to the twins' incomplete understanding of the events—led to chaos in their stories. Symbolically titled "Paradise Pickles and Preserves" the first chapter hints at the terrible experiences the twins have been through, reveals three deaths and suggests that the story that had happened in a number of hours has been preserved for twenty three years for a new narration.

> That a few dozen hours can affect the outcome of whole lifetimes. And that when they do, those few dozen hours, . . . must be resurrected from the ruins and examined. Preserved. Accounted for. Little events, ordinary things, smashed and reconstituted. Imbued

> with new meaning. Suddenly they become the bleached bones of a story. (32-33)

With adult hindsight, Rahel's perception of past events uncovers the real stories behind the official ones, to make the family's "hidden morality" emerge "to the surface and float a little while. In clear view. For everyone to see," (35) once again, but with other skeletons to expose. Rahel unearths the symbols of Estha's inability to testify to the truth which she finds in the "Wisdom Exercise Notebooks" they had used as children. Estha is nameless, and therefore cannot give his version of the events as he belongs to a hybrid space, begotten in an intercommunity, interreligious love marriage and living with a divorced mother who has not yet made her choice between her husband's or her father's name.

> On the front of the book, Estha had rubbed out his surname with spit and taken half the paper with it. Over the whole mess, he had written in pencil Un-known. Esthappen Un-known. His surname postponed for the Time Being, while Ammu chose between her husband's name and her father's. (156)

Furthermore, his essay on traffic and accidents reflects Ammu's own prophetic forebodings of the possibility of people hurting her children and her future, inadequate protection of them.

> If you go on the pavement . . . but on the main road there is so much traffic that they can easily knock you down and make you *senseless* or a *cripple*. (157)

> To Ammu her twins seemed like a pair of small bewildered frogs engrossed in each other's company, lolloping arm in arm down a highway full of hurtling traffic. Entirely oblivious of what trucks can do to frogs. (43)

It is now for Rahel to fiercely watch over Estha. For this, she needs to return Estha to his mind through their joint memories so that he can at last accept his participation in the tragedy for what it really was and not for the treachery he had imagined it to be.

2. Time-Shift, a Postmodern Strategy

(a) Past and Present

Time-shift, associated with a narration in the third person, is used as a postmodernist strategy of rewriting,[2] using the official version as a palimpsest to uncover hidden truth. Indeed, the artificial construction of the text with the constant backward and forward shift in time is a means of re-establishing the truth as well as order in the twins' lives. The shifts in time are linked to shifts in point of view as we have the opposing perceptions of the seven-year-old twins and of the adults, in the interpretation or relation of events. This link between time and viewpoint allows the narrator to gain the reader's sympathy by revealing which of the two groups are unreliable narrators of the stories contained in the main narrative through a cunning juxtaposition of the children's incomplete understanding of what is being recorded by adults and the faithful depiction of the scenes they have witnessed and which belie the adult narrative. Official history becomes a story related by powerful people who apply double standards to others in relation to their belonging to a particular gender or caste. The personal histories related in the narrative are opposed to official history, which is used as vellum on which the narrator inscribes critical comments on laws, rules, values and notions of decency.

It is Rahel's smouldering anger that pushes her to constantly shift between past and present in order to reveal the horror behind the official version of the police so that Estha can travel twenty-three years back to disentangle his role as an unknowing victim from that of the different adult perpetrators of Velutha's cruel death and perhaps move on with his life. It is her re-visiting of the past that juxtaposes the perception and silent witnessing of the events by the twins alongside the adults' re-arranged and interpreted version of the same events. Time had been the principal obstacle, enemy to the twins, either stuck on a toy watch or moving forward relentlessly so that when they try to set right what had gone wrong, they discover it is too late, as Velutha is dead and the Inspector and Baby have already registered their version of the deaths of Sophie and Velutha. The narrator needs to master this element to rewrite the true story by relying on the twins' memories.

(b) Future and Timelessness

Throughout the novel, time is perceived by the twins and their mother as a threatening element which crushes personal stories to inscribe collective history on them. The future holds nothing but worrying possibilities for the twins. From the very moment the twins meet their cousin—indeed even before she arrives in India if one takes into consideration the week of rehearsals—their lives change as they are relegated to the second or inferior position their great-aunt so anxiously wishes to see them in. Their confrontation with the white child in the "Indo-British contest for the best behaviour" leads them to their first loss. Estha's disobedience leads to the apprehension of a fearful future that holds the menace of punishment. He dreads the word "Layter," which like a sentence pronounced in court is split into two hammering syllables "Lay. Ter," reminding us of the ominous sounding "Dum. Dum," that echoes through the book accompanying dark happenings and their fears.

> And later became a horrible, menacing, goose-bumpy word. Lay. Ter. Like a deep-sounding bell in a mossy well. (145-46)

The future is not kind to the lovers either. Velutha's entrance into the "Touchable" world is a chance event that should not have occurred and is described as "Madness [that] slunk in through a chink in History. It took only a moment" (214), for the laws that forbid him entry into the world that controls history go back to ancient times, even before the English came to India. No wonder Ammu can meet him only at night when all the sentinels of the traditional world are asleep, adding even further distance between her world and his as she rows across the river to reach his territory. (333-34) Margaret Kochamma herself belongs to the English working class and yet has no memory of Velutha's face.

> Strangely, the person that Margaret Kochamma never thought about was Velutha. Of him she had no memory at all. Not even what he looked like. (264)

Velutha is thus symbolically cast out of time, left to the a-historical fate of an untouchable that neither Indian nor English history will acknowledge.

> He left no footprints in sand, no ripples in water, no image in mirrors. (265)

The History House, near which Ammu and Velutha meet is out of time, where crimes can be committed in the name of religious history/stories without needing to be recorded or accounted for in society. The children's presence while Velutha is barbarously beaten by the policemen is a sad coincidence of hybrid children witnessing an outcast's death, whose toy watch indicates that they cannot counter Baby Kochamma's false FIR (First Information Report).

> The watch they all forgot. It stayed behind in the History House. In the back verandah. A faulty record of time. Ten to two. (312)

The twins' own time and version of the events are left behind in the veranda of the History House to be buried by the rains. Their childhood world of painted watches and fairy tales cruelly keeps them out of "Real Life" (5) except when Baby Kochamma cleverly weaves a fiction to bully them to participate in it and thus definitely alter their reality and lives before they realize the extent of their great-aunt's treachery. This then is time as it had been lived by the lovers and the twins, unalterably moving towards their undoing.

When Ammu is insulted by Police Inspector, Thomas Mathew, who tells her that the police do not take statements from prostitutes and their illegitimate children (8), he has revealed to her the position she will hold in the future. Ammu, through her sexual union with an untouchable has erased her past of belonging to the powerful and wealthy and has become as vulnerable as Velutha who does not leave the imprint of his footsteps behind him. Even though Ammu has the knowledge that her lover had been killed for having defied tradition and the social order upheld by the members of the higher castes, she does not immediately realise that her future will be the same as Velutha's because she has been assimilated to his caste and therefore has become invisible in society. When Mammachi in sheer rage tells Velutha that she will have him killed he answers quietly, "we'll see about that" (284) because he himself naively believes that the "walking backwards" days were over. Yet, his brutal murder reveals the ingrained belief in India that inter-caste marriages, sex are more than taboo, they are considered as a transgression of the religious laws that are to preserve the purity of the high-caste. So when Ammu tells the Inspector, that "she'd see about that" (8), her future will be identical to Velutha's which reveals that the defiance of tradition is punishable by death as in ancient India. Velutha's body is dumped into the pauper's pit by the police who use it regularly, the reader is told, hinting at the number of people who pay with their lives certain transgressions (321). In the same manner, Ammu is incinerated as the church refuses to bury her for her transgressions of the same rules. The incineration is a manner of blotting out her existence which can no longer be recognised by the high-caste as she has become an outcaste by transgressing the line that separates her world from Velutha's.

> The threshold is a real as well as a symbolic bar marking a critical transition. . . . For women, a step over the bar is an act of transgression. Having committed that act, they may never re-enter their

> designated first world and must live by their irretrievable choice of making the other world their permanent space.[3]

Just as Velutha cannot leave the trace of his footsteps on the sand, Ammu's body is reduced to ashes, echoing her fears of a dead future as revealed in the repetition of negatives in the narrator's description of her despair of an arid future for herself.

> No milestones marked its progress. No trees grew along it. No. (224)

Ammu's loss is total as preordained by the religious laws. Manu's precepts state that a high-caste man can marry a lower-caste woman and elevate her to his caste while a high-caste woman loses her caste by doing the same and Ammu's short love affair with Velutha has led to the application of these laws that go far back into India's past.

(c) Circular Time Structure: Trap or Hope

Faced with the fact that neither the Inspector nor Baby Kochamma are objective or truthful, the reader is forced to reflect on the veracity or validity of other, official versions of history, of laws and of the narrators of these law books. The placement of the love scene at the end of the novel just as the incestuous scene is, becomes a comment on the right to love, on the necessity to transgress certain laws that meddle with the very happiness of people in the name of religion or social order. The tragic lives of the twins, their mother and Velutha are vellum on which the narrator inscribes a strong criticism of religion, history or laws as they are practised by people. Faced with the lyrical depiction of Ammu and Velutha's love, the reader, bearing in mind their cruel fate, is made to see that the beauty of love is worth the struggle, for the promise of a better future. Ammu's love is revealed as the starting point of the tragedy on a small-scale level, but the ingredients for the making of such a tragedy, the narrator says, go back to the ancient laws of India and perhaps carry in them countless other stories that had been crushed by official versions.

> Equally, it could be argued that it began thousand of years ago. . . . It could be argued that it began long before Christianity arrived in a boat and seeped into Kerala like tea from a teabag. That it really began in the days when the Love Laws were made. The laws that lay down who should be loved, and how. And how much. (33)

The reference is to the *Manavadharmashastra*, or *Laws of Manu*, and reveals that whatever her choice may have been Ammu was bound to lose. Manu proffers that a man does not lose his status by marrying a woman of a lower caste but that a woman loses her status in the same case. A woman can marry a man of her own choice but in that case she loses the right to the jewellery her parents have gathered for her dowry. Little wonder then that the jewellery that Ammu, and then Rahel are entitled to, is heaped on the aged, virgin grand aunt who followed the rules. But if Father Mulligan and Margaret Kochamma are untouchables in an orthodox Brahmin interpretation of the religious laws, then the narrator reveals the double standards with which certain people are punished for the very same acts that others can undertake amidst general toleration and even secret admiration, like Chacko's manly needs that lead Mammachi to build him a separate entrance to his room so that the factory workers who satisfy them need not walk through her house.

Rahel's re-memberings return Estha to his mind at the end of the narrative and also change the tragic end of her mother's love story to a promise of continuation. The last word of the novel is "Tomorrow," and hindsight shows us that the future was destructive, for matters only got worse as for example, the Inspector's gross behaviour to Ammu when she tried to prove that Velutha was innocent.

> Later, when the real story reached Inspector Thomas Mathew, the fact that what the Paravan had taken from the Touchable Kingdom

> had not been snatched but given, concerned him deeply . . . and he tapped her breasts with a baton. . . . It was a premeditated gesture, calculated to humiliate and terrorize her. An attempt to instill order into a world gone wrong. (259-60)

But it is also Rahel's memory which re-orders the narrative and places her mother's love scene at the end, with the promise of another meeting between the two lovers. The inescapable, tragic end of Velutha and Ammu is thus relegated into the midst of the novel by the narrator who symbolically places the coming together of the two at the formal end of the novel in an effort to allow that forbidden love to live on in her own narrative. David Lodge points out the difficulty of admitting certain losses.

> It is the inexorable, unidirectional movement of time that makes life tragic in our human perspective, unless one believes in an eternity in which time is redeemed, and its effects reversed. (78)

The struggle, then, is worth the tragedy as Velutha feels even after dreading what punishment he was going to receive on the seeping out of their story. "*Things will get worse*, he thought to himself. *Then better*" (290). Indeed, through the double time pattern she chooses for the novel, Roy drives in her point: the a-historical Love Laws cannot erase the chronology of the lives of the characters despite the violence of history's henchmen. Velutha, one of the principal characters, is presented as a "God of Small Things" (330), who has to obey to the "Big God [who] howled like a hot wind, and demanded obeisance." (19). Despite the weight of this giant tradition (religion), it is the individual's chronology which is imposed on the timeless laws and more, the linearity is broken by the narrator who imposes the encounter of the lovers at the formal end of the novel.

Time is a central girder in the novel, all the elements of the story relying on it. It is through the preservation of memories that the truth is revealed twenty-three years later and that personal stories are reconstructed, in defiance of official history.

Paradoxically, Rahel's toy watch, which had kept them out of history, also keeps the memory of her mother alive and the truth intact until she unearths it like some magic potion that will revive Estha's mind. A second transgression of the Love Laws through incest serves to set free Estha's and Rahel's "hideous grief" and long-stifled pain as Estha can finally admit "the reason for his silence" (12) after Rahel removes the "inky tranquillizer on his past" (12). This had been made possible only through the constant time-shift in order to reveal by contrast that the adults' version of the history was as tainted by their perception of the world as the twins' understanding of it was partial. The remembering undeniably shows that certain events cannot logically lead to others. If Velutha was murdered, it was only because of Baby Kochamma's jealousy of Ammu and her resentment of the twins' carefree attitude, when, according to her, they should have displayed some unhappiness, and most of all, because of her hatred of Velutha whom she irrationally and wrongly holds as responsible for her humiliation during a Marxist demonstration. This leads us to compare the degree of reliability of Baby Kochamma or Inspector Thomas Mathews with that of the twins as narrators of the underlying narratives.

3. Unreliable Narrators and Polyphony

One must first mention that the point of view colouring the major part of the narration is Rahel's. We are given an almost first-hand account even of Estha's separate experiences like the taste of his sandwiches which Rahel can taste, as her memory is kept awake unlike Estha's anaesthetised one. She can however awaken him to the outside world and moreover, Estha knows that his sister has come home even before he reaches the Ayemenem house.

> It had been quiet in Estha's mind until Rahel came. . . . The world, locked out for years, suddenly flooded in, and now Estha couldn't hear himself for the noise. (14-15)

Rahel and Estha are described as having joint identities and a single Siamese soul, thus granting Rahel the authority for the revisiting of the whole story with details of facts she had not witnessed as she "shares other memories too that she has no right to have." (2) Accuracy and faithful depiction are ensured as they share the same mind in a sense.

> Now, these years later, Rahel has a memory of waking up one night giggling at Estha's funny dream. (2)

Objectively speaking, the twins are unreliable narrators of the sub-narratives, as for example their relation of what occurred in the police station, as they are not only part of the narrative, but are also inexperienced when the most important events take place: their understanding of the world is partial. Moreover, the world and events are coloured by their moods as the factory becomes "angry coloured" when Rahel, jealous of the attention paid to Sophie Mol, puts her red plastic glasses on. But the novel's narratives are multi-layered, containing several stories in one, several voices behind Rahel's. Rahel's memories as an adult hold in them her own story as a child, her brother's, her mother's Velutha's, etc., and it is mostly her vision of the events that the narrator presents us with. The unfair presentation of events and the criminal act that the police had committed have already been grasped by the twins who are unhappily tricked by their vengeful aunt and are not in a position to impose their voice. Their reading of the policemen's signboard listing the police's qualities, backwards, is symbolically placed at the moment when the police's cover-up of the murder (with Baby Kochamma's help) is taking place. Estha is chosen to participate in the distortion of the truth which is to be registered. There is need then for Rahel to go back in time to clarify certain things that they did not grasp as seven-year-olds, like the necessity of their mother's presence in such a situation. The twins only had a sense of the injustice without a clear understanding of the adults' motives or of the whole picture as is revealed by their ignorance of the meaning of the phrase that Inspector Mathew declares to their mother in his coarse Kottayam dialect.

> The Kottayam Police didn't take statements from veshyas or their illegitimate children. (8)

But their witnessing of the scenes is brought back accurately by Rahel who associates these unquestionable images with her observations. An instance of this is the opposition between Baby Kochamma's presentation of the love affair between Velutha and Ammu as "attempted rape" which when discovered by Inspector Thomas Mathew, results in the sexual humiliation of Ammu. This sexual violence Ammu is subjected to by the very same Inspector, is a means of terrorising her into silence.

> 'If I were you,' he said, 'I'd go home quietly.' Then he tapped her breasts with his baton. Gently. *Tap, tap.* (8)

The narrator's comment is a means of rehabilitating Rahel's dead mother and of commenting upon the sorry state of justice, and the meaning of decency. Ammu's courage and honesty are rewarded with violence from the very guardians of justice. Moreover, the Inspector's twisted morality makes him condemn a sexual relationship between two lovers because of social hierarchy but allows him to use bad language and even sexual harassment of a mother in front of her children.

> Inspector Thomas Mathew seemed to know whom he could pick on and whom he couldn't. Policemen have that instinct. (8)

Baby Kochamma's self-righteous indignation at Ammu's misbehaviour is opposed to her blackmailing the twins to choose between two lies. They are forced to choose between "the story she was telling them" (317) in which they were the murderers of Sophie Mol, and the lie in which their beloved Velutha was the villain who had kidnapped them and caused the death of their cousin. The only participation they are allowed to have is to answer by a single word "Yes" in order for the aunt to contain their voices. The burden of that treachery leads Estha to aphasia until Rahel comes to leaven the weight of the terrible guilt he feels in relation to Velutha's murder as well as his own mother's death, "His fault. [. . .] Because he was the one who had said it. But Ammu that will be never!" (325)

Baby Kochamma's bad faith is cleverly exposed by the narrator's revelation of the double standards in the application of the caste rules. It is Rahel's voice that dryly comments on Baby Kochamma's affectation through her use of the words "schoolgirl shudder" (257) to convey the latter's disgust and inability to understand how Ammu could stand the smell of an untouchable. The narrator/Rahel's sly comment reveals Baby Kochamma's hypocritical interpretation of religious laws to suit her ends.

> And she shuddered theatrically, like a child being force-fed spinach. She preferred an Irish-Jesuit smell to a particular Paravan smell. (78)

In India any Brahmin knows that in a strict application of Brahmin rules, Father Mulligan is as untouchable as Velutha. This orthodox separation between castes is still existent for certain people, as is revealed by Mammachi's disgust at Margaret Kochamma's working-class cheapness.

The children's belonging to a hybrid space makes them castaways and, in a certain sense this entitles them to narrate the stories of people belonging to other minority groups, like Velutha or the Kathakali dancers, who are likewise used by the upper-caste Hindu capitalists. From their hybrid vantage point, the twins can appreciate Kathakali Ballet to which they are introduced by Comrade (Pillai) as well as the Anglo-Saxon literary tradition, as they belong to a family of anglophiles (52). Their wide education leads them to try to make Miss Mitten, Baby Kochamma's Australian missionary friend, learn what palindromes are and appreciate the fun of reading backwards, "Malayalam" and "Madam, I'm Adam" (60). Unhappily, just as she does not bother to check which language is spoken in the place she is going to, Miss Mitten cannot believe the twins can teach her anything as her attitude that is based only on assumptions about the Third World reveals. She offers the twins a "baby book—*The Adventures of Susie Squirrel*," (59) presuming that the level of English, Indian children would speak was lower than the white English-speaking world's, when ironically the twins have read a children's version of *The Tempest* that Sophie Mol their English cousin older than them by two years has never heard of despite her living in the so-called first world, England, thus starting on the wrong foot with the bright twins. She also presumes that the language spoken in Kerala was "Keralese," causing Estha to declare that her impression was a "Highly Stupid Impression" 60). Miss Mitten's deluded idea of a mission to backward children in the Third World leads to her inability to accept that she could learn something new from the twins.

This equals Baby Kochamma's supposition that Sophie Mol would know Shakespeare or her frantic need to prove herself worthy of the colonising race and to "Set herself apart from the Sweeper Class," (144) by insistently quoting Shakespeare to Sophie Mol, are all instances that prove the unreliability of adults who lie to themselves. Baby Kochamma equally manages to persuade herself that it was Velutha who humiliated her during the Marxist demonstration while Estha refuses "to seek refuge in fiction" (311), rejecting Rahel's offer of veiling the truth who one can say in passing plays the role of a kind of second mother to Estha (protecting him until she actually grows into her mother's skin) with Velutha's imaginary brother even when he witnesses the barbarity with which the police beat Velutha up. 'It isn't him, Rahel whispered to Estha. 'I can tell. It's his twin brother. Urumban. From Kochi' (311). The only instance in which Estha seeks to fictionalise reality is when he sees Velutha dying in the police station and yet chooses to betray him to save his own mother, as the savagery of the scene added to his forced participation in this macabre version of official history is unbearable. 'You were right. It wasn't him. It was Urumban' (320). However, it takes two pills of Calmpose for each of the twins, administered by Baby Kochamma, for them to accept self-delusion and believe that Velutha escaped to Africa, unlike their great aunt, who lies to herself wide awake. Yet the next morning they reveal the truth to their mother. However Ammu is unable to record her version of the events as the Inspector declares the police do not accept F.I.R.s from prostitutes and their illegitimate children. The serious-sounding administrative abbreviation F.I.R. for First Information Report is a sarcastic comment on the imaginary nature of the 'facts' that are recorded. Estha, who was the one chosen to answer the question whether he recognised Velutha as their abductor, has already erased his surname and, thus is in a position in which he cannot give his own version. He can only be used to confirm the version of the ferocious guardians of 'tradition.'

> Over the whole mess, he had written in pencil *Un-known*. Esthappen Un-known. His surname postponed for the Time Being, while Ammu chose between her husband's name and her father's. Next to *Class* it said: 6 *years*. Next to *Subject* it said: *Story-writing*. (156-57)

Only those who abide by the rules, and who are admitted by tradition are allowed to speak. Ammu and her twins symbolically have no name for the "Time Being" and thus share the same unrecognised space as Untouchables who cannot leave a trace on history.

NOTES

1. This chapter draws from a paper presented at the SAES conference in Metz, France in 2002 and has been published as "Re-membering Personal History in *The God of Small Things*," "Palimpsest"

Vol. 25, No. 1, Autumn 2002 in *Commonwealth Essays and Studies*.

2. See chapter entitled 'Time-Shift' in David Lodge, *The Art of Fiction* (London: Penguin, 1992).
3. Malashri Lal, *The Law of the Threshold. Women Writers in Indian English* (Simla: Indian Institute of Advanced Study, 1995), p. 12.

Chapter IV

A Woman's Narrative

Considering its semi-autobiographical element, the novel appears as an attempt to retrieve the voice and the power that lacked those of its protagonists because of age or gender, in order to set right their history. This explains why the narrative is mostly coloured by the female protagonist Rahel, and relies on the vivid and imaged language of children.

1. Through the Red Plastic Glasses

The narration is mostly coloured by Rahel's perception and emotions as symbolised in the colouring of the external world. The factory, or the world, become red coloured or "angry coloured" through her plastic glasses. The similes, metaphors and the twists to the narrative thread are all therefore related to Rahel's emotions. Even when Rahel's anger does not permeate the narrative, the similes or metaphors foreshadow the role she is going to play as for example in her unearthing the hidden secrets through the linking of the violent monsoon rain with her arrival in Ayemenem.

The imagery on the first page describes an abundant fecundity and simultaneously alludes to the decaying of an overripe fruit that cannot be consummated. The renewal that Rahel is going to bring with her does not contain a ready-made solution to regenerate her twin brother's lost youth and innocence. So, the 'decay' is too far set in for Rahel to totally save her brother. Also, the jackfruit that bursts and the overripe mangoes that the crows gorge on, are part of the whole setting in which the slack, sloppy characters—Baby Kochamma and Kochu Maria—that the reader is just going to be introduced to, live. They exemplify lost possibilities and wasted lives, promises of happiness that fester like an unattended wound, that parasites—the crows—feed on. Trapped in this bogged environment is her own twin brother for whom she has returned from America. The image of abundance leading to decay reveals the general state of the house and the mentality of its occupants. Nothing has changed apart from the deeper sinking into tradition, habit, a slow death just as the family's wealth had led to its bankruptcy. Baby Kochamma's life is wasted because of an impossible love; Kochu Maria works only to have her wages collected by her brother-in-law and the factory was used by Comrade Pillai until it goes bankrupt.

From the outside, one can see that the house and the garden are unkempt, reflecting the keepers' lack of former interest and diligence in the maintenance of their outward appearance. Baby Kochamma had at first replaced her love for Father Mulligan by growing exotic plants that she had learned to arrange and grow in America. Now, Father Mulligan being dead and the family's reputation being beyond the point of salvation, she has turned to television, ready-made images replacing the reality of the outside world, for even the windows are opened with parsimony. The unkempt garden and the mossy walls are indicators of the family's loss of interest in maintaining their image of respectability as even inside the house, insects' corpses litter even the interior of the house. Decay has attained the core of the family.

Whether it is used in personal histories or in official history, the colour red indicates the price paid for every attempt at change. The colour red is indeed associated to blood, bloodshed and the recurring theme of lost innocence or ruined childhood in the novel. The image of the communist party's flag in front of Comrade Pillai's house, "The red had bled away" (13), reminds the reader of the sacrifices made in the hope of attaining equality and reveals the ebbing of the force from this party in India as the initial exaltation led to total disillusion. The poor discovered at their expense that the communist party was to secure the position of those already in power, to equally distribute the power and wealth between the already rich and not between the untouchables.

In the same manner, private lives are crushed in order to uphold tradition. Ammu, who has gone against the sacred biological laws by polluting her high-caste body with an untouchable, is punished through her motherhood for she dared deviate from the path traced for her by generations of women before her who accepted their bad fate in good faith. Ammu, whose walk changed from a "safe mother-walk to another wilder sort of walk" (44) is chased out of Ayememen and dies alone in a cheap motel. "Rahel saw that her eyes were a redly dead." (31)

The red colour in her eyes not only reflects the crying and the strain she had gone through, but also symbolically foreshadows her cruel death. She dies because she is unable to breathe and one of Ammu's eyes with a bloated and blue pouch testify to this struggle for life. In the same manner, this red colour testifies to Ammu's refusal to accept what Baby Kochamma has apparently given in to, living a sexless life as it is the colour of the wedding sari. The decision Estha makes, and that becomes a secret that they share and it is described as "A red, tender mango-shaped secret in a vat," a "Red Agenda" (200) that they will follow to their destruction.

The jaunty tone and cruel humour used to describe Estha's lost childhood and innocence in the words "ex-nun" only serve as a weapon for the grown Rahel to keep the pain at bay in order to maintain control over her memories. We should keep in mind that the story is related through her vision, the jauntiness serving as a buffer against the pain she still feels for her brother's trauma and as a mental defence against the random distribution of fate's blows to human life. The grotesque and the absurd way of presenting a child's terror and silent horror at having been molested by an adult through the use of the simile of an imaginary orange that is to be carefully held, calls to mind the image of the oranges that represent Christmas with its gifts for children. Indeed all the rhymes and songs that constitute the world of the child are linked in this novel to traumatic events.[1]

If the novel is semi-autobiographical and presents an adult view of childhood traumas, there is single line in it that can reveal that narrative distance is not always equalled with the dark humour with which these events are presented, and it concerns Rahel's "irrational' fear of an ordinary figure in the middle-class scene. "Sturdy was a terrible word. Like a dwarf's name. Sturdy Koshy Oommen—a pleasant, middle-class, God-fearing dwarf with low knees and a side-parting" (46). A child's fears do not leave him despite his apparent forgetting of a negative incident, thus the fears are revived every time an action or word reminds the child of the danger she or he has faced. If one compares Estha's reaction to the word "lucky" to Rahel's reaction to the word "sturdy" then the preceding premise can be confirmed in the logic of the narrative. Similar to the feeling that the word 'sturdy' evokes in Rahel, the word 'lucky' revives Estha's dread of the Lemondrink man, "'Lucky,' Sophie Mol said. Lucky rich boy with porketmunny. And a grandmother's factory to inherit. No worries" (150). Both Estha's silence about the abuse and the female narrator's casual throwing in of a single sentence concerning the word 'sturdy' without any apparent link to the immediate events might be compared to and considered as a hint to the sexual abuse of Rahel. They could be linked with the various clues that the narrator throws in a deludingly anarchic manner concerning adult violence towards children in all forms to reveal how negative forces in real life can hurt a child to the unhappy oblivion of his/her family. It may partly explain the writer's fierce attachment to defend the weak due to personal experience of a vulnerable position from where the weak subject's voice cannot be heard.

> When I was living alone, it happened when I was working as an architect. I used to be so frightened. One man was an inspector-general of police—he had all these medals—and I was scared because if anything had happened, it was my word against his, and you can see what they'd say: 'She's some weirdo living alone, with no family; look at the way she dresses.[2]

This silencing of the child, whose word can hardly have weight, particularly when the predator is a decent member of society or even of the family, can be equated with the apparent meaninglessness of this sentence, which seems to carry no explanation, no cause and effect. Just as the child's fears of its molester are difficult to convey, the text graphically reproduces the reception of the child's attempts at conveying what happened to it, especially as this perverted sexuality is something it does not understand and therefore cannot easily put into words. Thus the sentence concerning a respectable middle-class dwarf appears in relation to the word 'sturdy.' Indeed, in real life, a child's declaration, or hints at any abuse that it has suffered can come in the midst of other worries of the surrounding adults and thus pass unnoticed or be given no weight. Estha's misadventure is totally missed by Ammu, and likewise the sentence concerning Rahel's fear in relation to the word "sturdy" appears with no apparent link, conveying the impossibility of defending oneself when one is small and helpless in the face of a malevolent predator. This idea of surface respectability that hides predators and the invisibility of molested children could be an echo of a part of Roy's interview with Maya Jaggi. Arundhati Roy was sexually molested as a child by a grandfather figure. "I didn't know what he'd done, but anyway, there was no way people would believe me. Everyone called him Pappachi. But it's not unusual; it happens a lot."[3]

2. Proximity to Nature

The four elements are extremely important in Roy's novel. The author herself has declared that she has grown up close to nature; therefore it is only natural that nature's presence permeates the lives of the characters and reveals itself to participate in their very functioning, such as the twins' physical need for their river. These natural elements exist in a conflicting, opposing mode, the one destroying and the other saving or at least rehabilitating, underlining the tragedies lived by the main characters and serving the author's various purposes such as her political ones as revealed in her activism.

• Water

The author's present crusading against the building of dams that would destroy the nature in her native country is a proof of the importance she gives this vital element. Water, by which the family's tragedies started, permeates the setting from the damp mud under Estha's shoes (15) to the damp moss-grown walls (1) of the house, habit having rendered Baby Kochamma and Kochu Maria indifferent to the filth and the decay around them. The paper of the letter, which accompanied Estha when she was re-Returned (9), has grown soft due to the dampness in the air and indicates the state in which Estha's mind is, and above all, symbolises his fate which equals the letter's as his father has sent him back to get sucked in the quagmire of the antiquated house and its aged occupants.

The metaphor of rain as the "silver ropes ploughing up the earth like gunfire" on the very first page, is representative of Rahel's harsh revival of the bad memories in Estha's anaesthetised mind which awakes to the sounds of the outside world only when his sister comes back to Ayememen. It is Rahel's arrival that unearths the hidden stories under the official story, just as the rain ploughs the earth. Indeed, one learns that "It had been quiet in Estha's head until Rahel came. [. . .] The world, locked out for years suddenly *flooded* in." (14-15, my italics) Ammu, Rahel and Estha love the river and love by the river which they use to live their various loves and lives. The twins are indeed tightly linked to the liquid element as their birth is described as an act of swimming into the world, "(swimming) through their lovely mother's cunt" (93) and continue to be at ease in this element as their Uncle Chacko teaches them to swim from a tender age, so that they know their limits in relation to this element.

Water is a central element in the novel, because it is felt as such by the twins, "water always helps" (108). It is the means to offer a psychological boost to a person crushed by traumatic events. The imagery linked to water and to the pattern of the lives of the little family also forms a narrative thread whether it refers to tragic events that undo the family, or whether it reveals that water is the element of comfort that they resort to when in anguish.

The four major characters are linked to each other through this liquid element. Velutha is described as belonging to the water world that is the river Meenachal (333) and Ammu licks the drops of the river off his body. The twins dream of their river (122). When Ammu indulges in moments of rare pleasure, she has midnight swims (44).

When they cross into forbidden territory where history is inscribed, they cross the river, a liquid border that separates their lives in a space where they are approximately carefree children to the other side where they witness horror. There is a parallel in the roles played between the mythological river Styx and the Meenachal. The belief that the dead had to cross some barrier that divided the land of the living from that of the dead existed in many religions. The Greeks and Romans believed that the dead were ferried across an infernal river, the Acheron or Styx, by a demonic boatman called Charon, for whose payment a coin was placed in the mouth of the deceased, and Sophie Mol dies holding a silver thimble for luck in her clenched hand (251). Nevertheless this silver currency does not bring peace to the twins who accompany Sophie through this journey across the river that turns infernal. Their lives had come to an end even if they survived the boat accident, "Not Death. Just the end of living" (321).

The evocation of dams flooding (15) accompanies Rahel's return, for it brings back the unbearable memories which gush violently into Estha's mind after he had learnt to carefully shut the world out. But like the metaphor of rain unearthing reveals, her return brings with it a liberation which necessitates a passage through the pain that they had denied themselves by a feeling of guilt. Sophie Mol drowns in the water though as she does not really belong to this world as Estha and Rahel do. Sophie Mol who blackmails the twins into taking her with them, for she wishes to be part of their group, had in fact negotiated her own death. Her cruel fate reflects in a manner another instance of what seems to be reverse colonialism or the case of the issues of interracial marriages as developed under the title 'Hybridity.' The Western characters who come to exploit the native resources, also end up being engulfed by 'The Heart of Darkness'; Sai Karippeu dies a first time of love for his young native lover, and then a second time when his ghost is pinned to a tree by a sickle by Vellya Paapen. The tourists who come to profit of cheap hotels and ethnic ballets are in fact victims of a MacDonald's system but where neither the native nor themselves gain. Surrounded by the stench of the dying river where their countries invested money to help India and which in fact kills its natural resources, the tourists of the first world are surrounded by the ugliness resulting from their aid to third world countries.

Similarly, Sophie Mol who has a powerful position, "Loved from the beginning," forces the twins to take her with them to her own loss. The river, in a sense, appears to return the unkindness of the West by its cruelty.

• Fire

Fire is an important metaphor in the novel, and is mainly associated with loss and death. From the first chapter, the story or tragedy that is to be told is evoked in the image of burned, destroyed objects.

> Perhaps it is true [. . .] that a few dozen hours can affect the outcome of whole lifetimes. [. . .] like the salvaged remains of a *burned* house—the *charred* clock, the *singed* photograph, the *scorched* furniture—must be resurrected from the ruins and examined. (32, my italics)

The house, the memories are also evoked as burned, charred objects, corpses. The inflatable goose, a toy, is significantly burned by a policeman's cigarette (91), putting an end to the twins' innocence. The innocent victims of marriages are likened to polished firewood by Ammu who sees the elaborate wedding preparations as a meaningless and useless effort, for her own experience of marriage was a short but intensely unpleasant one (44). Ammu's referring to marriage as being led to the gallows however applies less to her than to the victims of arranged marriages as she chose her husband. Arranged marriages are still a very common practice in India, coming after endless dowry negotiations and comparisons of horoscopes only to result in some cases in the 'accidental' burning of the bride if the total amount of dowry money is not paid. Every year, around 800 to 1000 women are 'accidentally' burned while cooking.

The cremation of Ammu is foreshadowed in the link between her own description of herself in the photograph of her wedding "Like polishing firewood" (44) and the narrator's description of Ammu on the day she and Velutha feel the attraction that proves fatal to them, "Her shoulders . . . shone as though they had been polished." (45)

The moths that appear "like strange ideas" and that burn themselves on baby Kochamma's bulbs that are dim, can be assimilated to the small, fragile, new ideas of Velutha, Ammu and her children and of their small attempts to change things in the traditional society they live in. On the other hand, the corpses of the insects that litter the floor to Baby Kochamma's and Kochu Maria's indifference indicate the number of lives sacrificed in order to preserve tradition. Baby Kochamma and Kochu Maria are the two remaining representatives of tradition. Symbolically described as aged and physically repulsive, they are still alive after having consumed all around them. Indeed, the raging fire that Rahel observes when the furnace of the incinerator is opened refers to the cleansing Hindu rites, yet this incineration is practised on a Christian woman. The incineration of Ammu's body like the Hindus is resorted to, not for religious reasons but because the society casts her away like a pariah containing a catching disease and that the other members of society should be saved from. The heat, the fire are likened to a beast (163) reminding us of the human sacrifices that were made to divinities in order to save the rest of the society. Thus one can assimilate caste fears to an ancient, irrational fear and the reaction to Ammu's choice to live as she intends to as superstitious and pointless.

• Earth

The most obvious metaphor is that of the Earth woman, against whose life man's life and destiny are paradoxically rendered more than insignificant as it is man who supposedly 'reigns' on earth. Yet, compared to earth's life, the whole history of humanity itself dwindles down from the length of time perceived in words like History, and Civilisation to a mere couple of hours in the life of the universe. The parallel between man's insignificance compared to earth can also be applied to an individual's life in comparison to the history of a nation, or a civilisation for the narrator painstakingly reveals the importance of the smallest details in an individual's life. This is how the narrator sets the his/story of an individual against the History of a nation to give more importance to the smallest things as they count more, like the happiness in dreams that can count if the dream brings real pleasure.

Sophie Mol and all that she represents, through her belonging to the caste of the former rulers of India and to the rich first world, is reduced to dust by nature. "Dus to dus to dus to dus to dus" (7), even though the memory of her loss is kept alive and erases the lives of the twins. A dead U.K. child is kept 'alive' in the family's memories as she is considered more important than the Indian twins. Likewise, the toy watch, a symbol of another version of unrecorded history, is buried in the earth by the monsoon rains every year. Nevertheless, this means that whatever is out of sight is not forgotten but can be kept, preserved, and it is for the protagonists of each story to learn how to unravel every (sub)story and explain it by contrasting it against other histories. But the grown Rahel will set things right by 'bringing to life' a buried history from the very earth that concealed it.

As Eros and Thanatos are clearly revealed to be closely intertwined in this tale much more than any other, earth offers life and removes it. Ammu and Velutha's affair, the best proof of life and Eros, starts on a piece of earth, which seems to be prepared by the twins, "a boat-shaped patch of bare dry earth, cleared and ready for love." (336) So finally, there is some hope for Estha and Rahel, as the earth lets loose one of the buried secrets, thus joining the mood of the last pages that end on a hopeful 'tomorrow.'

• Air

Air as atmosphere generally envelops the characters in a negative way, underlining the unpleasant or dark side of the events. The image of the insects that burn themselves and transform the air, the atmosphere around an adult Rahel, "The Air smelled of something burning" (10) are evocative of the fate reserved to Ammu who was incinerated, reduced to ashes just as anything that comes against Baby Kochamma's ideas and the traditions that the latter defends, traditions represented by her dim bulbs. The forty-watt bulbs are equally another metaphor for her mind which is fixed in an ancient order. When Ammu snubs Margaret Kochamma when the latter reveals her ignorance and tendency to stereotype Orientals, the animosity between Ammu and her brother fills the air. "But the Waiting Air grew Angry." (179)

The twins, like Velutha, merge with the natural elements as the following quote reveals. Estha, who as soon as they return from the airport goes into the factory to prepare himself in case he is tracked down by his molester, fuses the atmosphere with his fear and the need to prepare himself. This atmosphere is perceived and reflected by Rahel who feels from inside the house that her brother is waiting for her.

> Outside, the Air was *Alert* and *Bright* and *Hot*. Rahel lay next to Ammu, *wide awake*. . . . She could hear the blue cross-stitch afternoon [. . .] and Estha waiting for her. (201)

Rahel is thus in total symbiosis with the well-known nature around her and thus can "hear" her brother waiting for her just as she feels the other happenings that are enumerated, and when she joins him, they find the boat together which indicate their keen sensitivity to their surroundings and especially to each other.

The repetition of approximately the same sentence becomes a clue that gives the reader the means to interpret the incest as an act of defiance of the laws that led their mother to her death or, as a 'biological' necessity, love for the adults and a Siamese oneness for the twins. During the scene of incest that takes place between the twins the air is described as quiet as before a storm, "Except perhaps that it was a little cold. A little wet. But very quiet. The Air" (328). The other forbidden act of love between their mother and the untouchable man takes place in a calm environment before their deaths, "It was a little cold. A little wet. A little quiet. The Air" (338). The breaking of the love laws is the only means for the twins to revive the memory of their mother and to experience the grief that they had put away due to the guilt that their aunt had implanted in them as children.

> Only that once again they broke the love Laws. That lay down who should be loved. And how. And how much. (328)

The dampness of the monsoon air in Ayemenem seems to permeate the memories and take the harshness off certain events, so that memories can at last be let loose as with the passing of time they seem to have lost their cutting edge. Yet, this air also reveals the mushy condition into which the weight of memories has put the house in, from the memory of Sophie Mol's loss:

> The paper had grown soft, and folded like cloth. She had forgotten how damp the monsoon air in Ayemenem could be. Swollen cupboards creaked. Locked windows burst open. Books got soft and wavy between their covers. (9)

Never has setting been so intimately linked to its story and characters. As Roy herself has claimed that her writing is deeply affected by her life in Ayemenem's nature as a child,[4] one can understand the symbiotic link and narration of the twins' lives in the novel with that of the nature around them.

3. East is Best

Most things loathed or deeply criticised in the novel are presented as pertaining to the West and what is considered as its 'modernity.' Kochu Maria whom the twins loathe and whom the narrator clearly presents at her most disadvantageous is assimilated to a "bottled foetus . . . in a biology laboratory" (162), while the nasty inquisitiveness of Comrade Pillai is "like a searchlight" (130) and "plastic bags," a Western invention, litter the twins' beloved river, and "factory effluents" pollute it (124-25). Pappachi, the Anglophile, beats Ammu with an object linked to Westerners' use of particular garb for equitation. "He flogged her with his ivory-handled riding crop." (181) Cynthia vanden Driesen lists a few more examples of Western objects presented in a negative light in her article.[5] Sometimes, even when not presented as badly influencing, the West appears ugly. The love song that coincides with Ammu's realisation of her wish to join Velutha is presented as a "cheap coincidence" (332). Working abroad is also a dehumanising and miserable experience, as with the 'gulf' workers, and Rahel's American experience. All in all, Roy seems to say the East or home is best.

The most important of the Western imports that are negative is the bank loans that destroy the local nature. Keeping in mind that the history of the earth can be telescoped into the life of a human being, a woman, the history of Kerala itself would take a smaller period of time. The twenty-three years that have passed by since the time when the twins swam in the river and rowed across it, become almost an instant in Kerala's history. Considering the history of the river which offered a living to generations of fishermen, in what appears to be the blink of an eye, the twins' river, the Meenachal, and the life in it have been suffocated with "pesticides bought with World Bank loans" (13). Therefore, the representation of the earth as woman could also serve to reveal the incredibly short span of time needed by man to ruin nature. The case of the Meenachal mirrors the author's combat against the building of dam. Roy is against the privatising of natural resources and packaging and selling what belongs to the peasants of the regions through and imported economic system from the West, if it is not the Westerners themselves who make deals with the governments of the East to exploit their natural resources.[6]

On the individual level, although Chacko's propositioning these women is no different than Hollick's attempted seduction of Ammu, the objects of his desire arc never presented as anything more than shadowy, giggling figures which might lead to the interpretation of this presentation as proof of a certain ambiguity in the author's stance. Thus a first interpretation would be that Roy herself is not entirely capable of escaping her own, class-based position and that she silences these particular women whom she represents. Their plight in being not only exploited as a labour force but also in their dignity as humans as they are forced to prostitution by the combined factors of their economic and social position and this does not seem to be given as much weight as Velutha's story. The fact that they had not been murdered for having defied the social order like Velutha did, seems at first to diminish the horror of their exploitation as human beings, and appears to remove from them the tragic cloak of victimisation that Velutha is clad in. Yet the trade of the body in all forms is one of the worst forms of alienation a human being can experience. Roy is not a stranger to combating this form of exploitation and degradation of the soul as with her reference to the cheap porn magazines dangling in the shop, pornography in this form being a Western import, and more courageous, in her attack of Shekhar Kapur with the case of Phoolan Devi in an article by putting into script the rape of a living woman.[7]

In a text where the symbol of the exploited lower class labourer in the character of Velutha is exalted to the point of rendering him too dangerously and romantically perfect for an intensely realistic novel, it appears suspect that the female figures who are exploited are presented as almost shallow figures. Yet one must concede that the narration is deliberately light in the presentation of Estha's molestation too. Therefore, the fact of presenting the female workers as giggling figures underlines the nature of Chacko's exploitation of 'innocent' or barely educated women, along with the realistic reference that they had families to feed, reveals their lack of choice and thus underlines a fate perhaps as cruel as Velutha's on certain levels. The seduction of the female factory workers should rather be read as a comment on the absurd adaptation of imported theories, as Chacko's interest in 'discussing' with his employees is based only on the beauty of the women. The omniscient narrator's comments on Chacko's self-satisfied, self-representation of his 'discussions' as evidence of his Marxist soul, through the addition of information on the bases of his choices of one female comrade over the other, are clearly denunciations of exploitation. Then, Roy's apparent presentation of the women as giggling nitwits is a fierce comment on the way women are subjected to pressure and exploitation. Indeed, limiting their voices to giggling and announcing that "Chacko Saar" had arrived is perhaps a means to underline the extent into which their spirits have been bent and not just point out a sexually submissive behaviour. The parallel between their silent, even active acceptance of all forms of exploitation, their total servitude, can be made with the black slaves' wish to please the master, and their loyalty to the white master in the southern states of the United States before the abolition of slavery because they have no other means of survival.

Rahel's hinting to the problem of classification and the management of pickles is another example of the criticism of the thoughtless imitation of the West in a manner that halts progress. The Food Products Organisation's attempt to control the enterprises by patenting and classifying diverse products results in Mammachi's producing banana jam that sold despite its being an 'unauthorised' produce due to its non-conformity to government specifications. The adult Rahel's comment 'As per their books' (30) states the sheer idiosyncrasy of certain laws and regulations.

In the same manner, Chacko's importation of his Western knowledge is useless to the factory not only because he has studied literature and not management in England but also because of the interference of his personal dreams of landlordism. Chacko wrongly adapts Western marketing methods of registering the family enterprise as a partnership and takes on extravagant bank loans which lead to the bankruptcy of the profitable little family enterprise even though his mother had always successfully run it 'like a large kitchen' (57). The criticism here is not of the method in itself but of the inadequacy of certain methods when applied to the local market. Things get worse when Western methods are used to satisfy the personal interests of a privileged few. Chacko's local adaptation of Western democracy and Communism is expressed in his feudal methods. Voting is an act, an assertion of one's will, it is a choice that indicates its voters' independence and the choice of the modal "make" in this context clearly reveals the imposition of his will on helpless workers. He also appears to get only the female workers involved in the factory's business as they do not represent a real danger for his position. The omniscient narrator forays into his thoughts to reveal that Chacko's choice of the Comrades depends on the beauty of their hair.

> Once he even took a group of them to attend Trade Union classes that were held in Alleppey. They went by bus and returned by boat. They came back happy, with glass bangles and flowers in their hair. (65)

> He would hold elections for them. *Make* them vote. [. . .] He smiled at the idea of holding round-table negotiations with Comrade Sumathi, or, better still, Comrade Luckykutty, *who had the much nicer hair*. (122, my italics)

Ammu is not a dupe and she bluntly names her brother's exploitation of the women who have no choice.

> Ammu said it was all hogwash [. . .] a landlord forcing his attentions on women who depended on him for their livelihood. (65)

All that is adapted to Western standards, seems to be polluted, bringing with it decay, loss or petrifaction as in the way the Kathakali ballet dancer is described, his economic condition, "His velvet blouse has grown bald with use" (231) appearing to have made of him a half-willing slave to Western imperial economy due to the choices of those who run his country. Things have changed and the Kathakali dancer is frustrated in his art, because he has to cut down six-hour representations to adapt them to the tourists' fickle attention (231). The Kathakali dancer needs to dance in the temples devoid of an audience to beg forgiveness of the Gods he has sold for his mortal needs. This dancing is the desperate seeking of a refuge against the passing of time which has led to the partial loss of their identity through the trading of their culture and/or religion for survival.

> In Ayemenem the men danced as though they couldn't stop. Like children in a warm house sheltering from a storm. Refusing to emerge and acknowledge the weather. (234)

Indeed, things are no longer what they used to be even in the most sacred of an ordinary Indian's life—religion—as the narrator humorously points out in the scene where the sleeping priest is seen with "A brass platter of coins lay near his pillow like a comic strip illustration of his dreams." (228) However, the Kathakali dancers' attachment to their culture reveals that holding on to tradition holds in it a means of salvation, just as Rahel and Estha's attachment to their culture.

The narrator's occasional hints at the various evils that have befallen the Indian society make the novel a quasi-social pamphlet. From the World Bank loans to imported Marxism to satellite TV, all of which are Western additions to the Indian society, the narrator underlines that the way these have been introduced into India, or adapted to Indian society only bring social disorders and worsen the state of the Indian society.

4. Violating the Patriarchal (Literary) Tradition

Whether they are fathers, sons or brothers, the male characters in *The God of Small Things* are represented in a very negative light when they are not blotted out by the stronger female characters. Weak, infantile, the male character in this novel is portrayed as unable to undertake his role as a father and preferring to be mothered. The social position that he enjoys only serves to fulfil sexual desire and to spite or destroy the very females who nurture him, thus making him a dangerous Other for the female characters.

The endeavours of the male characters are qualified as clumsy and sterile as opposed to the creative capacities of the female characters who are the only strong and reliable figures for all those who are dependent: the working community relying on Paradise Pickles and Preserves, and the twins. Nevertheless, the mother figure is also compared to the sexually enterprising and also destructive goddess Kali, symbolically swallowing her son's testicles and therefore procreative powers, or at least ensuring her exclusive control in the field of parenthood. The mother figure is a not only a castrating one, she also seeks her own sexual fulfilment through the taking over of the son's sexuality as Sudhir Kakar points out, "In all societies the image of the 'bad mother' combines both the aggressively destroying and the sexually demanding themes." (90)

The relations between the male and female characters are conflictual as there is a struggle for control on financial, social or sexual issues. The outcome of the struggles is either castration or erasure of the male characters even though loss is paradoxically experienced mostly by the female characters. The only characters who experience close bonds devoid of violence are those who have no social status, the twins in their privileged brotherhood, Ammu the divorcee, and her Untouchable lover, Velutha. These characters are however destroyed, giving the reader a generally pessimistic view of the man-woman relationship in the novel's world.

(a) Female Creativity or Textual Domination?

The female characters are omnipresent in this novel, creating, building, but in a certain sense their uncomplaining toiling expunges the male characters' attempts at success and gives them a castrating aspect. The maternal connotations in the appellations of the female characters are no coincidence as the youngest girls are considered as potential mothers and variations and diminutives of the word 'Amma,' 'mother' are attached as suffixes to girls' first names. The Tamil word, 'Ammavaru,' means the primal mother and this novel, even if it underlines that women are limited to their roles as mothers, also points out the authority that motherhood confers on the woman. The twins are brought up, nurtured by various mother figures. Ammu, their own mother, is almost always designated by the only social function that is left to give her living space, for when her sexual desire is perceived, her person is split into two distinct figures, woman and mother separated, the two being incompatible.

> As though she had [. . .] Even her walk changed from a safe mother-walk to another wilder sort of walk. (44)

Even in the love scenes with Velutha her children are evoked by the female narrator and Velutha himself is perceived as a child by Ammu. Their Mammachi, or grandmother, is a reigning matriarch and from her youth, her name Sosha is transformed into Soshamma, 'Mother Sosha.' The other powerful female figure is Navomi Ipe, the twins' great-aunt, called Baby Kochamma, Kochamma signifies "Aunty," used for the aunt who is the younger sister of the parent. One could say that Baby Kochamma's title, "Aunty Baby" or the literal translation of "Kochamma" being "Small Mother," is a nebulous one which underlines the distorted nature of the life she has lived and is an irony as she has wasted her life as a woman, being neither wife nor mother but an obese great-aunt with a ludicrous name.

The male characters are blotted out in the female text as is indicated from the fact that Estha has deleted his name from his "Wisdom Exercise Notebooks" and it is only with the appearance of a female figure, Rahel, who unearths his childhood narrative when she returns from America, that his prophetic storywriting is revealed. The link between the erasure of the name from a notebook with the brand name "wisdom" and Estha's loss of mind can also be mentioned as a symbolic erasure of the male when represented in the female text. From Ammu's attempts at erasing the image of their father from the twins' minds by allowing them to look at his photograph only once, one can read her symbolic erasure of his legal right as a father, had he wanted it. This is further underlined in her refusal of using his name even temporarily for her twins while she unwillingly chooses between her husband's and her father's name. This refusal of the mother to adhere to the transmission of family name by the male is continued by the narrator; the text never mentions the name of the father and the world of the novel becomes an entirely feminine one that intentionally rejects men.

The narration is mostly coloured by Rahel's perception and emotions. The factory or the world becomes red coloured or "angry coloured" through her plastic glasses. The similes, metaphors and twists to the narrative thread are all related to Rahel's emotions and vision. Even when Rahel's anger does not permeate the narrative, the similes or metaphors foreshadow the role she is going to play, as in the allusion to her future unearthing of the hidden family secrets through the linking of the violent monsoon rain with her arrival in Ayemenem. The harsh but necessary revival of the bad memories in Estha's anaesthetised mind, which awakens to the outside world, occurs only when his sister comes back to Ayemenem. It also indicates that through Rahel's memories, the true facts of Ammu's story—in the possession of the female characters Baby Kochamma who hides it, and Ammu who is dead—are going to be revealed.

The only actions of the male characters that are mentioned are the destructive or the sterile ones. The male in the female text appears as a parasite, living off the woman's efforts and mistreating her at the same time. Velutha is an exception in his quality as an all-rounder succeeding in every enterprise he undertakes, almost making one wonder if the author has set her mind to sing the praise of the Dalits, if not the discreet consideration of a possibly existing figure in her past due to the semi-autobiographical nature of the novel. Velutha is the only male character who is totally devoid of malice. Velutha is written in the female text of Rahel's reminiscences as the only positive agent in their little family's lives. From the gifts he carves for Ammu as a talented child, to the short period of intense joy he gives her as a divorced and lonely woman, to his joining of the twins in their imaginary world of children's play with an ease and an intuition that their Oxford-educated uncle, Chacko sorely lacks, Velutha appears as a perfect figure. Even physically, Velutha is portrayed as manly, handsome and noble-minded, while Chacko is feminised as having "slack, womanish legs" (16).

Through Ammu's gaze that is revolted against the "smug [order of her] world" (176) Velutha's caste disappears and only his noble behaviour and the details of his physical beauty are perceived and used in order to equate him with his creative skills through the wood that he works, "She saw the ridges of muscle on Velutha's stomach [. . .] A swimmer-carpenter's body" (175). This description is contrasted with the scabs of the unmanly legs of her brother who represents the decaying past, the old order. Both Velutha's hopes for a future where "*walking backward days are over*" and their love are contained in Ammu's understanding of Velutha's body and what it represents.

> [Ammu] understood the quality of his beauty. How the wood he fashioned had fashioned him. Had given him his strength, his supple grace. (334)

An equation can be made between the beauty of his body and that of the little marvels that he used to carve and offer Ammu without his hand touching hers. As Ammu realises and appreciates the transference of the beauty of the little wooden toys to Velutha's physical body, Velutha realises that Ammu also has gifts to offer him. From the moment both realise that history's laws need not necessarily be respected, the physical link is made possible between the two despite the traditions. For fourteen nights the lovers share small things and an intense passion, indeed Velutha does not accept the rules of the past like his father, for he is not a "safe Paravan" and has carried with him from his past only hopes, not a slavish mentality. "His smile was the only piece of baggage that he had carried with him from boyhood to manhood." (175)

In contrast to Velutha's noble and manly attitude, Chacko behaves in a puerile and mean manner; he worries his scabs and displays his repugnant boils when visitors are around in a mean attempt to spite his mother and Baby Kochamma (248-49), his behaviour totally opposing his feudal pretences and his family's status. Velutha learns at the expense of his life that the communist party does not interfere in its member's private lives, but Rahel is back to reveal that it actually does when it suits its controlling members. Rahel's return to India and her role almost appear to continue what her mother did: rebel against the instilled order that thrives on the disruption of lives of the minorities, women, untouchables. The children's father is described as having unrefined behaviour, blowing spit-bubbles and "shivering" his legs (84). He has an 'effeminate' tendency to rely on his family—throughout the novel we see that it is the women who are the pillars of the family—and then on his wife in order to be kept in his job through her prostitution, all this in a society where men are traditionally supposed to be the bread-winners. In the end, the only element the twins have as a reminder of their father is a letter written in a woman's hand, his second wife's convent school handwriting (9). Velutha, on the contrary, possesses the gifts that the men of the family lack.

Both men of the higher castes, Chacko and Ammu's husband, significantly have something negative linked to their legs or feet. Just as the expression 'to have feet of clay' indicates a weakness, this image of having weak legs or probably nervously shaking the legs indicates that 'standing on one's feet' or behaving in a responsible way for one's family is what the two high-caste males lack.

Men's behaviour is spiteful, revealing an inner weakness and inadequacy when compared to their women, leading them to resort to violence and a mean tendency to ruin their companions' or close relatives' reputation. For instance, Pappachi's imaginary darning to make visitors think Mammachi neglects her wifely duties. This also reveals an aspect in the society the author wishes to criticise, which is the burdening of the woman with all the household chores even when she is the breadwinner.

Her husband, in order to intimidate her into prostituting herself to the English Manager, Mr. Hollick, so that the former may keep his job on the tea estate, subjects Ammu to drunken brawls. All the incidents linked to the male characters and (re)membered by Rahel are negative ones, leaving the reader to wonder if all the men of the family or of the higher castes are totally devoid of good feelings, talents or if the narrative is too coloured by Rahel's emotions to be reliable.

The excessively positive portrait of Velutha puts him in danger of being considered as a pure creation of an angry young woman in the feminine text, a text that could be considered as an act of solidarity between the women and the Dalits as marginal groups. The allusions to the various political and social issues dear to the author glut this novel which, had it not been written in such an original manner, would have read like a pamphlet. The instance of Ammu's not having the same inheritance rights as her brother is more than a mere allusion, for the author's mother, Mary Roy,[10] sued her brother concerning female inheritance and obtained a change in the inheritance laws in favour of the women in Kerala.

The text becomes an act of defiance to the age-old patriarchal tradition, which has led to the erasure of generations of untouchables from the history of India by giving a Paravan all the noble and enterprising qualities severely lacking in the high-caste members who loftily claim to be the sole possessors of positive qualities. This same, perhaps insistent, rehabilitation of women can be seen in the comparison of moral qualities and effective actions of both genders in the whole novel.

In the reality of the Indian society, erasure of the male cannot happen that easily, as it is woman who faces discriminations and violence of all sorts that place her either completely under the male power or symbolically on the threshold of the home, exiting the doorstep only to second the male in sustaining the family by her work. Woman's real field of influence is inside the home in the 'traditional spheres' of female activity for the major part of society as it is the case indeed in a great number of societies. The physical repression of the female by the male in the real world is answered by an obliteration of the male in the female text. The male characters are wiped out in various ways. The oldest matriarchal figure, Mammachi, blots out her husband as her pickling brings her social recognition unlike his discovery of a moth that belonged to a yet uncategorized species (49). The tradition of female figures getting unofficial social recognition continues when the workers address Mammachi instead of her Oxford-educated son, Chacko, despite his making his mother the "sleeping partner" and taking over the management of the factory. Mammachi is totally unconscious of her effacing of her husband and son, but her succumbing to Chacko's every demand is an unconscious means of keeping her son in a totally dependent position.

There is a positive interpretation of only one incident in which a female figure negates the presence of a male. When Rahel sees Velutha in the march, Ammu scolds her as she does not want her children to recognise him at this particular moment. This is not because she does not wish to show publicly that she knows an Untouchable, for Ammu is not hypocritically revolutionary like her brother while asserting her superiority over the factory workers. She might not consider herself above stating that they know an Untouchable, especially as she herself has no legal standing, no *locus standi*, or "Locust Stands I" being a woman. It would be meaningful that Ammu tries to protect Velutha through sheer sympathy for his status as an exploited worker and unrecognised talent. Truly, her own position is somewhat similar to Velutha's in the factory, for her hard work goes unrecognised and un-rewarded by her brother and by the laws as she and her children live in the Ayemenem house on sufferance. It is Baby Kochamma who keeps this incident in mind and uses it in order to obliterate Velutha as a representative of the 'Dalits' whom she considers as a potential threat to her class.

A second interpretation of this same incident would be Ammu's gradual recognition of her attraction towards Velutha and her refusal to admit it to herself from the fear that this recognition would lead to the risk of sliding into a dangerous relationship with him. Indeed, the day they return from the airport and Ammu dreams of the one-armed man during her nap, she refuses to use his name, thus unwillingly letting him slide out of the dream into the intimacy of her bedroom. This omission itself reveals an unconscious struggle with her feelings as made clear by the omniscient narrator.

> Somehow, by not mentioning his name, she knew that she had drawn him into the tousled intimacy of that blue cross-stitch afternoon [. . .] She knew who he was—the God of Loss, the God of Small Things. Of course she did. (220)

This second interpretation would make their affair more logical as it means that it would have started gradually by some obscure and unmanageable feelings of mutual attraction before the day Ammu and Velutha both realise they are actually going to make the relation physical, "He saw that . . . to give him too" (176-77), rather than have it start just the day they come back with Sophie

Mol, which would make the love affair seem rather like a narratorial device that serves the plot and climax of the novel.

In Rahel's adult recollections, her uncle Chacko is represented in a negative manner and even his Oxford education is ridiculed. The twins' misunderstanding of the phrase can be the key to a hidden truth. Rahel, as a child, has perhaps misunderstood her uncle's use of the Latin phrase *locus standi*. Pronounced in the British, not Latin manner, the words in the dialogue have been understood as three words, not two, locus standi, becomes locus stand I, with the "t" of standi being attached to the first word. Would the text then imply that the reader is to look deeper into the apparently excellent elocution of the so-called scholar from Oxford and more, to discern meaning in the apparently dyslexic representation of the phrase by a little girl grown into an academic failure? We have two layers of meaning; one of the member of the Shibboleth, Chacko who as a male has read at Oxford and whose pronunciation gives social recognition, and the other being the trapdoor that banishes its speakers out of sight. The first use of this phrase (57) holds its original Latin meaning of no 'legal standing' as it is situated in the context of Rahel's childhood and has been explained to the twins concerning the fact that their mother does not have the same rights to the home and the factory as their uncle. The author's allusion here is of course to the discriminatory laws that her own mother had faced and fought and which do not allow a woman to inherit like her brother, which explains why Chacko can chase his sister from her own parents' home after the tragedy.

There is an ironic allusion to the Indian tendency to resort to certain bookish words in English or in Latin that are viewed as markers of social importance and power, even when he or she does not really understand the words used as in the use of the Latin phrase "Locus Standi" (57 and 159). Any self-respecting Indian moviegoer knows that the posh hero resorts to exclamations and phrases in English whenever under the powerful influence of strong emotions like anger, love, for dramatic and important situations need to be stressed! Then perhaps the narrator is pointing out that Chacko, like some other high-class Indians, does not put into practice his costly education, and maybe does not understand everything that he has learnt in Oxford as might reveal his purposeless quotes of passages from books (38), making him a typical Brown Sahib, a mimic man. Chacko, who has "read at Oxford" (56), would have then made a pronunciation mistake when repeating the Latin phrase to his niece and nephew.

The second use of the Latin phrase takes on a different and palimpsestic meaning though, twenty-three years later, as it is an adult Rahel who remembers it on reading Estha's notebooks. If the Latin phrase is still used with a mistake, "locusts" retrieves its original meaning. Rahel's use of the negation "no locusts stand I" alludes to the falsity of her uncle's accusation that follows just after the Latin phrase, "Because Chacko said she had destroyed enough already" (159). If one is to take the meaning of the word 'locusts,' which is grasshoppers, and knowing that they travel in swarms stripping the areas that they pass of all vegetation, then one can read a second level of meaning in Rahel's deliberate repeating of the mistake. The meaning would be that the swarms who actually destroyed the family and who left a desert are the various members around the twins and their mother, and not Ammu. All the events are narrated through Rahel's perception. Therefore, the members of the family and the police, who act together in the making of this tragedy, can be perceived as swarms who destroy the lives of the twins and their mother, leaving an aridity in Estha's mind where "the dry season looked as though it would last forever" (10).

It is only in verbal aggression, and later, in the symbolic erasure of the male in the evidently feminine text of *The God of Small Things*, that woman can fight for her rights and retaliate to male violence and repression. However, this female retaliation is rejected as bickering by the male characters in power.

> 'Ammu,' Chacko said, his voice steady and deliberately casual, 'is it at all possible for you to prevent your washed-up cynicism from colouring everything? Silence filled the car [. . .] where it hurt. (70)

This prompt retaliation of Chacko's is an instance of censoring, for Ammu's remark all at once derides Chacko's ingratiating thanking of the striker—and also alludes to her similar position as an exploited worker. Chacko's remark reveals his fear in that explosive situation where they are all, as members of the owner class, vulnerable to attack from the thronging Marxist demonstrators around the car. Chacko's cool answer is meant to cast away Ammu's heavily significant observation as the insignificant squabbling of a bitter and disillusioned divorced female, thus silencing her critical voice and burying the truth of their situation, where Ammu and the other female members of the family work hard for Chacko to reap the social recognition and legal benefits. When female retaliation is effective it becomes far too destructive as it punishes the innocent and the offspring rather than the adult male. The narrator not only deprives the children's Baba, of a name—he is never named—but also of space as Ammu rarely refers to him. This erasure of the male to the extent of not naming him leaves the twins without a social space from which they can act. Estha is nameless, "Esthappen Un-known" (156), which deprives him of a full social identity, and therefore makes him unable to give an FIR at the police station. It has to be Rahel who saves Estha from his invisible, erased condition for "Estha occupied very little space in the world" (11).

The link between the erasure of the name from a notebook with the brand name "wisdom" and Estha's loss of mind can also be mentioned as a symbolic indication that the authoritative figure in the female text can only be a woman. Ammu erases the presence of their father by allowing the twins to look at his image only once. Her symbolic erasure of his legal right as a father (had he wanted it) comes through her refusal of using his name even for her twins. This refusal of the mother to acknowledge their father is continued by the narrator in whose text the name of the father is never mentioned, he is only called Baba, which means father.

(b) A Latticed Tale

The text is constructed by using the patriarchal literary and religious myths or scriptures as the foundations in order to reveal the narratives of women's lives; that in their contradictory and repetitious nature are like so many hollow spaces behind a thick wall, proof of a hidden cavity which the patriarchal text covers. For example, behind the *Manavadharmashastra*'s prejudices against women and untouchables and its precepts of the management of these two subordinate groups by resourceful men battling against female depravity and general unreliability, the events in the novel build an intricate design where, behind the façade of male enterprise, lie numerous sacrifices and exploitation of the female. The female mothers the male in the image of the self-sacrificing feminine figure that is generally recognised in India. These beliefs and prejudices which are perpetrated by men and women of the older generation, are opposed to facts that reconstruct the truth of the lives that are narrated through Rahel's perception with her belated hindsight. This new narration at least reveals the schism between the truth of the various lives, as lived by the women, and the self-delusive methods used by them in order to respect traditions and yet find comfort in their pre-ordered lives. For example, Baby Kochamma's love and therefore life have been contained because of her inability to surpass the male literary and religious traditions that divide the Roman Catholics and the Orthodox Syrian Christians. Her own narrative of her past struggles to contain her love within the accepted limits due to her position as high-caste unmarried girl but is (re)membered by Rahel who reveals the real reasons behind the myth of her "sacrifice." Her sacrificed love represented by the exotic garden she has created by toiling in the heat of afternoons is only a bitter attempt to possess the 'exotic' monk that she had not been able to seduce and to make their imaginary love thrive in the soil of her mind. Her cultivation is a form of suffering as she works in the heat of the afternoons even though no one really benefits from her sacrifice. Her bitter reactions to Ammu's revolt against her fate as a divorcee are reproaches that point out her own noble sacrifice in the name of the family's honour and position in the community as she advocates self-effacement in the face of ostracism.

When the narrator relates her story, it starts from the statement of Baby Kochamma's lost life as a woman, to travel backwards to the foundations of that lost life, which lie in religion, but religion as in the peculiar Indian amalgamation of Hinduism and Christianity. The narrator shifts from the relation of Baby Kochamma acting out the life of a young bride at eighty-three to the narration of the causes of her lost love, which lie in the "folklore" of her father's status as a Blessed One that acts as an extra pressure on her life as a woman. The narration travels backwards moving through the intricate design of criss-crossed events that remind us of the lattice windows that served to hide women from the public eye, making it possible to imagine her ideally and to (mis)represent the same woman more than once in man's imagination. For indeed, it is Baby Kochamma's strong-headedness that leads her to the adoption of a religious conviction that opposes her father's, who is moreover a high representative of the faith that she deserts. This conversion earns her a reputation that prevents her from finding a husband and ironically prevents her later on even from sharing the same faith as the man for whom all her desperate enterprise had originally been undertaken, as he becomes a Vaishnava.

Religion, with its symbolic father figure in the Patriarch—as head of the Orthodox Church—is belittled by the narrator, together with its sacred myths, for the halo of Baby's father as the "Little Blessed One" is revealed as originating in a humorous incident in which the act of blessing is desacralized. If the halo of rulers and of belonging to a high-caste is kept aglow by the older members of the family, Ammu's fears reveal that ironically their inheritance due to inbreeding is not a serene holiness but a high risk of mental disorders (223).

The architecture of the text uses the foundations of the patriarchal literary myth that is perpetrated even by women of the older generation in order to reconstruct the truth of the lives while re-narrating them. Under Baby Kochamma's cloak of piousness and indignation at Ammu's display of pleasure or revolt that she perceives as immorality, is a feeling of resentment and jealousy. When the narrator relates her story however, it starts from the statement of her lost life, to travel backwards to the foundations of that lost life which lies in religion. The narrator shifts from the relation of Baby Kochamma acting out the life of a young bride at eighty-three to the narration of the causes of her lost love, thus underlining her past vain attempts rather than any personal choice in the lonely life she had led. The narrator links this tragedy to ancient India. The parts of the Kathakali ballet that are mentioned can be read as a parallel to Rahel's avenging role. Keeping in mind that Velutha is presented in a far more noble manner, and his unsuitability for Ammu, one can relate his position to the Hindu mythology in the following sentence:

> Kunti revealed her secret to Karna on the riverbank.

A mere reminder of the story of Karna can show the probable echoes in the characters' lives, here Velutha's tragic story, in his defiance of the law and winning of the princess and eventually in his betrayal by his communist 'brother' Comrade Pillai which leads to his death.

Kunti, the daughter of Sura, a Yadava chief, had been seduced by the Sun-God, Surya who had been taken in by her beauty. Afraid of the disgrace, Kunti asked to get her virginity again and Surya granted her request and made her a virgin anew, after she had given birth to a son, Karna. Kunti abandoned her son on the banks of the river, Yamuna, where a childless couple found him. The couple, a charioteer (Adhirata or Nandana) and his wife, Radha brought Karna up. Two incidents explain the episode of Kunti's pleading with Arjuna mentioned in the novel. First, Arjuna's skill in the use of arms makes him win in a grand tournament in the court of Hastinapur against Arjuna. But when asked to give his lineage, Karna, believing he is only the son of a lowly charioteer, refuses. The king's son, Duryodhana, declares however that only deeds ennoble a person, reminding the court that the Pandava princes themselves had been born out of wedlock. Indeed when Kunti later married King Pandu, she had turned to three deities to get her children as her husband Pandu had been cursed by a Rishi for the latter had received an arrow while he and his wife were making love in the woods disguised as deer. The three deities Kunti called to get sons were, Dharma, (a Rishi sage) considered as one of the Prajapati 'Lord of all Creatures,' a title applied to major divinities like Brahma, Indra, also employed to designate the Maharishis (born of the spirit of Brahma) to conceive Yudhishthira; Vayu, the Vedic God of Wind, to conceive Bhima; and Indra, at first Lord of Atmosphere and weather, then God of Lightning and Thunder, rain and dew, and then God of War, to conceive Arjuna. Duryodhana then bestows on Karna the title of Raja of Anga (Bengal) and crowns him. Yet Karna's caste keeps following him and divests him of everything he earns. The second instance of Karna's humiliation is princess Draupadi's Swayamvara, or contest during which a princess chooses her husband amongst various princes. The contest consisted in bending a great bow that no warrior had yet been able to bend. Karna easily wins but is rejected by Draupadi on the basis of his supposedly low birth, only to witness her choosing Arjuna who manages to bend the bow just after him. Ever since, these two humiliations burned Karna's heart and when the Pandavas went to war against the Kauravas, Karna who is on the Kaurava side against his own half-brothers at last gets the chance to fight against Arjuna. In order to save her children, Kunti then reveals her long-hidden secret to Karna; that he is her eldest son, and thus the older brother of his sworn enemies, the Pandavas. Kunti tries in vain to convince him that he should not fight the Pandavas. However, he rejects her advice and eventually becomes the commander of the Kaurava army arrayed against his brothers, the Pandavas. Karna is eventually slain by his brother Arjuna.

As for Draupadi's proud and passionate nature one can see her reflected in Ammu's defiant nature as well as in the purpose of Rahel's return which turns out to be finally a means to bring the family's "hidden secrets out in the clear for everyone to see." Draupadi washes her hair with blood while the bones of the story that the narrator puts together clearly serve to avenge.

> Bhima disembowelled Dushasana and bathed Draupadi's hair in his blood.

In the *Mahabharata*, an apocalyptic world-spanning war is triggered when the five Pandava brothers foolishly wager their joint wife, Draupadi, in a rigged game of chance against their enemies, the Kauravas. Arjun had won Draupadi's hand in the contest but had wished his eldest brother, Yudhishthira to take her as his wife. The origin of this polyandry lies in the Pandava brothers' mother, Pritha, unknowingly telling her sons on their return home to share whatever they had won. Her words being law to them, Draupadi became their common wife. Dushasana, one of the most important Kauravas, is responsible for dragging Draupadi forward just after their side has won her and attempting to strip her naked though this attempt is foiled by a miracle for every time her saree is unravelled another one appeared. Bhima, the second of the Pandava brothers married to Draupadi, and especially noted for his strength (he was the rival of Dushasana in wrestling prowess), swears to take vengeance on Dushasana by drinking his blood. Draupadi, the most notable woman in Hindu legend for her proud, passionate and vengeful nature, however, claims vengeance and wishes to bathe her hair in Dushasana's blood, she declares she will not fasten or wash her hair until she is avenged and her wish is fulfilled. Toward the end of the climactic battle, Bhima exacts the revenge described in this passage, and in the process killing a man who, like all the Kauravas, is his cousin.

As a conclusion, one can say that the whole novel is the narrative of an "angry young woman" where writing appears as a means of avenging the repressed and particularly the repressed female in various ways. The main character's vision and the narration almost blend for the humanistic telos of the narrative. Dark as the novel may seem, the ending stresses the closeness of the twins and leavens the weight of the narrated events. The closeness of brotherhood seems to be the answer to the turmoil of life for we know that Rahel has come back from America to take care of Estha and that she has managed to shake him out of his catatonic state. For indeed it is only after her unearthing of his Wisdom notebook that we have Estha's perception once again in the description of the grown-up Rahel which reminds us of the description of Ammu's cremation coloured by Rahel's pain.

> She was lovely to him. Her hair. Her cheeks. [. . .] A beautiful, *hurt* mouth. Their beautiful mother's mouth, Estha thought. Ammu's mouth. (299-300, my italics)

Estha is released through the kiss that Rahel as a surrogate mother deposes on his hand like his mother's parting kiss twenty-three years earlier (300, 327). Incest, doubled by the fact that Estha sees his mother in his sister, is a means of defying those who destroyed their family, by retrieving their "Joint Identity," and also a sharing of their grief and strength. The physical closeness of the twins through the one incestuous relationship they have appears as a means to compensate for their having been cruelly separated and retrieve their oneness repeatedly stated in the image of the stacked spoons.

> That the emptiness in one twin was only a version of the quietness in the other. That the two things fitted together. Like stacked spoons. Like familiar lovers' bodies. (20)
>
> Only that Quietness and Emptiness fitted together like stacked spoons. (328)

The ending is not a classical one where all the knots are eased in a few pages, as it ends on a past event, the love scene between Ammu and Velutha, the chronological ending being the twins' grief. Nevertheless, the settings around them have not changed, the Ayemenem house being the very embodiment of stasis, leaving the reader to wonder what will become of the twins.

NOTES

1. See Vanessa Guignery for a study of allusions, quotes and other inter-intra textual references. *Le Spectre des Voix dans The God of Small Things*. In François Gallix, Arundhati Roy: *The God of Small Things—L'hybridité célébrée*. Paris: Mallard Éditions. Collection Angloscopies, 2002.
2. Maya Jaggi, "*An Unsuitable Girl,*" *Electronic Mail & Guardian.* Review of Books.
3. *Ibid.*
4. 'I'd never have guessed the book I'd write would be so full of earth, water, sky, insects. It's a surprise; there's so much underlife in the book. On every page, there's a god of small things. I love the earth there, and the landscape, with an emotion I find hard to un-

derstand myself. I remember everything—the smells, the fishing—so clearly, it's scary.' Qtd. Maya Jaggi.

5. Cynthia vanden Driesen, "When Language Dances: The Subversive Power of Roy's Text in *The God of Small Things*" in Dhawan.
6. See the author's articles in the books or Internet articles and interviews quoted in the bibliography.
7. Arundhati Roy, *The Great Indian Rape Trick.*
8. See Internet page http://www.rediff.com/news/sep/18arun.htm by George Iype 'Rediff on the Net,' for Mary Roy's struggle and victory to change the inheritance laws in favour of women in the state of Kerala.

Chapter V

Language and Power

Language is another factor that allows for a nation to be contained by a foreign power, or the various social groups in a nation by a dominant community. Roy's novel treats both aspects of the theme in a subversive manner as she either appropriates or reinterprets the Western culture. She also comments upon the Indians' use of the literature bestowed upon them by the English as well upon the similarity with which the higher castes who once had been under the English power in their turn keep the lower castes under control.

1. Intertextuality

Bhabha questions the idea that mimicry be an act of homage to the coloniser. The word homage indeed indicates respect and admiration, but relying on recent theories of language which underline that the process of communication can never be perfect Bhabha reveals how there is a wedge between what is said and what is heard or understood. The consequence is that the seeming adoption of the oppressor's discourse can in reality be a rejection of it.

> [T]he authority of that mode of colonial discourse that I have called mimicry is therefore stricken by an indeterminacy: mimicry emerges as the representation of a difference that is itself a process of disavowal. Mimicry, is thus the sign of a double articulation; a complex strategy of reform, regulation and discipline, which 'appropriates' the Other as it visualizes power.[1]

(a) Direct Quotation and Allusion

There are a range of historical and literary allusions that either become an ironical extension of the Westerner's or Orientalist's negative perception of India, thus commenting upon the narrowness of those holding these Orientalist views, or which are subverted to take on the opposite meaning in the context of the novel. In addition to the humorous dimension given to the perception of the Westernised returnees of their own families, there is an ironical use of almost every historical or literary allusion such as the use of Conrad's *Heart of Darkness*. This subvertive use of Western canonical texts holds in it the appropriation of the Orient by the West. However Roy does not limit her perception of the world she describes to a Manichean opposition of interests and values.[2] For example, the stone kangaroos that Rahel perceives as living, animated animals, present a significant reading of the signposts. The sign that is wobbled by the kangaroo is the one that indicates the taking over of the Indians of their own economy, in an initiative to make money out of their culture. It says: "Kerala Development Corporation Welcomes You," and has a Kathakali dancer doing a Namaste (139). All that was left of the Indian culture from that which had been transformed, reinvented, or revalorised. The narrator points out that it is so only when the aspects of culture are considered worth revalorising by the Western eyes, and so is used to allure the tourists into their own illusion of what India is. In this sense, the tourist trade is no longer that much the epitome of the exploitation of the East by the West than it is the means through which the East reappropriates some measure of control over its economy. This reading may seem a bit far-fetched until we realise that palindromes follow a certain pattern in the novel and are not haphazardly scattered, thus making all of the twins' readings and perceptions clues for the readers to follow the narrator's retrospective narrative.

There are two signboards that Rahel notices in the airport and the one that is steady, is the one that bears an ambiguous welcome sentence for it is read backwards. "Welcome to the Spice Coast of India." (39) Even if the board names Kerala as the place for which India had originally been colonised, for trading purposes, and indirectly refers to it as the coast through which Christianity and the Western world percolated India, it is read backwards by Rahel, thus indicating that one can invert what is stated. This reminds us of the twins reading the police sign backwards in a moment when values are upturned and an innocent man is killed in the name of a hypocritical maintaining of 'morality.' Thus the first is that Margaret and her daughter Sophie are not welcome by Rahel and Estha, for Rahel does fear Chacko will not love them anymore. Both twins have been punished so as to speak only in English, thus making Sophie's arrival associated with unpleasant things. There is a clue to this as Sophie Mol's appearance in the airport lobby produces a rush of hostile feelings in Rahel that she lets out by pinching her twin, "Rahel, overcome by excitement and resentment pinched Estha hard." (142)

It also indicates that the place where Margaret Kochamma is going to enter is no longer the spice coast which England is exploiting, but rather the place which serves Western tourists truncated ballets in the midst of a pestilent smell of Western-initiated aids that only succeeded in making the place regress. The musical *The Sound of Music* might have been chosen for the mere coincidence of the date but in it the adult narrator ridicules the protagonists of the movie that the anglophile family love. The nuns, traditional figures of piousness and honesty are portrayed as sneaking to their mother reverend, and in a sense are equalled to Baby Kochamma who tells tales to the 'Modalali' Mammachi to have Velutha and Ammu punished. Captain Von Trapp, the authoritarian figure, reminds us of Chacko even though the latter ridicules him by calling him Captain Von Clapp Trapp (98) just as Chacko is belittled by his sister and later on by his niece[3] for claptrap means rubbish. The link can be made with the empty thorax of the dead spider that Velutha baptises "Lord Rubbish," (339) if one reads the captain and the cloak of dead spider as symbols of a past empire and a caste system, both struggling to survive and impose their presence on the future generations. The fact that it is someone considered inferior to a family which places itself on an inferior level to the 'ruler race,' adds to the ironic comment of the narrator. The house named 'The Heart of Darkness' and the Kathakali dance can thus become a comment on the West becoming a victim to its own system of globalising, packaging and rendering exotic the core of the other's culture and identity but falling prey to marketing and capitalistic exploitation as with the hollow signs saying "Traditional Bridal Dowry Box" (126). Yet things are not as simple as one could imagine for it is not a simplified case of the Empire striking back. In Roy's novel, there do not seem to be any clearly defined winners or losers in this game of exploitation, for the Kathakali dancers also suffer from the very trade that allows them to earn a living.

2. Oxford Pickled in Kerala

(a) English as a Tool for Power

Apart from their hereditary professions inherited from one generation to another because of the caste-system, the linguistic features that they share link the various castes together and almost necessarily against each other. English being the language of the powerful, all the characters use it as a means of asserting their power over one another. Roy does more than offer a new brand of Indian English to the Western reader; in fact, it is not her priority. The play on language also serves to render in a jaunty tone certain sombre events without missing the possibility of laughing while all the while heightening their terrible nature, as the obvious laughter that the accent of the Orangedrink

Lemondrink man might provoke "porketmunny?' (102), despite his hateful appearance to the abused Estha, or the description of the abuse itself.

However, the novel also being about the joys that the twins and their mother live before they experience the most tragic events, thus certain events or thoughts are reported espousing the children's consciousness or perception of the world. For example, there is an instance of the narrator giving us a glimpse into Rahel's mind while she is in the toilets of the theatre, Abhilash Talkies. When her mother encourages her to urinate, we understand that the sound sets off thoughts in her mind. "Sssss for the sound of soo-so. Mmmmm for the sound of Myoozick." (95)

As Raja Rao had stated long time back (see Introduction) Indians adopted the English language and adapted it to their local life, colouring it with their experience. In addition to this, Roy has coloured her language with the children's perception and comprehension of the rules of the English, thus giving not just pleasure in reading but also a deep sense of reality, of entering the world the twins inhabit by making the reader see them in the process of acquisition of the language. We are given the child Rahel's perception of language when she is scolded by her mother, "Until Ammu shook her and told her to Stoppit and she Stoppited." Roy obviously also takes liberties with the English language because of her own love of the English language and her delight in experimenting with it for the sake of creating amusing rhymes (300), "Meeters from the Met, and Greeters from the Gret" (142). This last sentence makes us think of her informal education where reading and apparently enjoying studying was Mary Roy's ambition as a teacher.

All the innovations and techniques employed are in fact not merely reflective of an Indian's particular use of the English language, they indicate the social and economic position of the characters, education, power and even the ideological stances of some of the characters. Thus one-word sentences, topicalisation, emphasis and italics, capitalisation, subject-less sentences, faulty spellings, adjectival clusters, deviation from correct syntax, coining of words and change of parts of speech all serve the author's purpose such as reflecting the twins' powerlessness, Baby's snobbery in general and her sycophantic behaviour towards anyone English in particular, Chacko's Brown Sahib attitude, and Ammu's dry wit.

On the other hand, when Malayalam is used, there is a departure from power and prestige issues. English is used by Comrade Pillai as a proof of his status as when he mentions Sudha's "meeting with fracture," despite his dubious mastery of the language. It is actually the very proof of his inferiority on the educational level to Chacko for he feels that the words "my dear fellow" were an insult that Chacko addressed to him due to the latter's certainty that he, Pillai, would not understand it was an insult. So Pillai uses Malayalam when he wishes to underline his being on a same or friendly level with Chacko, when he tries to warn Chacko against letting a Paravan work in his factory (263).

Two other people separated by their caste from their childhood also use Malayalam when the power divide is bridged by their illicit affair. Velutha who had to place his gifts on Ammu's palm so as not to touch her is now given a tryst by a single word, "Naaley." The lack of precision concerning the lovers' trysts conveys the closeness they achieved in such a short period of time; a closeness also revealed by their use of Malayalam when they discuss the spider and other small objects during their nightly meetings.

• Capitalisation, Italics

Italics are used for emphasis, but also to indicate a second meaning or irony in the use of a word.

In the case of the epitaph for Sophie, the phrase is in Italics. "*Dus to dus to dus to dus to dus.*" (7) Though it is necessary that the phrases come from the Bible as they are Christian, it could be a comment from the author on the excessive use of English rather than Malayalam that supposedly sets the family apart from the 'uneducated rabble.'

Power is symbolised through a reference to the law even if it is mostly twisted to suit the perverse interpretations of the various characters. The police hide behind official letters like the important-sounding, official character of the abbreviation FIR for First Information Report when all they do is embroider a tale designed to mask their crime.

In order to paralyse and thus keep Estha under his power, for he has already decided to abuse him, the Lemondrink man resorts to the use of "legal" English to dissuade Estha from reporting the whole incident to anyone. "'It has to be a secret because drinks are not allowed before the interval. It's a Theatre Offence.' 'Cognizable,' he added after a pause" (103). The capitalising of the words "Written Complaint" (102) indicate the knowledge shared by victim and predator of the official and judiciary means to corner Estha and are a way the Lemondrink man indicates his stronger position to Estha. Thus, Estha is doubly bound by the fact that he feels soiled and therefore responsible for what happened to him like almost all victims of sexual abuse, as well as the fact that he had accepted a drink, though it was forced on him, when it was an illegal act. Both acts are thus to be kept secret.

Capitalisation also serves to warn, underline the danger of something, stressing its risky nature. Estha's fears of the Lemondrink man are revealed in the capitalisation of the word, "Anything." The word englobes all the unimagined horrors a child can be exposed to. On the other hand, the family's fears, reflecting any small community's fears of an unmarried woman in every part of India, are encased in the capitalised words, "Unsafe Edge" (44) and their wariness of her when they sensed her restless and therefore explosive moods, "it was best to just Let Her Be" (45).

• Topicalisation, One-Word Sentences and Subjectless Sentences

The effect of topicalisation, or "Thematic reordering" whether it be "thematic fronting" or "Thematic postponement," is to assign greater importance to the element concerned (subject, object).[4] In the instance of adding a sentence to explicit Estha's aphasia, the narrator uses this technique, "Stopped talking altogether, that is" (10), in order to convey the gravity of his withdrawal into himself after the trauma he goes through. This will later be explained by his guilt at having testified against Velutha. Similarly, the sentence "'Heritage,' the hotel was called" is a dry comment on the inverted use of the "ancestral homes" (126) a true heritage, for tourism, where the old subservient colonial relation is replaced by a new subservience as the natives play exotic modernising in a deforming manner their rich past traded for food. Indeed, what had meant a lot emotionally to past people is labelled with tags that indicate more of an empty cliché than a real and valuable information and guidance to the culture.

> They were labelled with edifying placards which said *Traditional Kerala Umbrella* and *Traditional Bridal Dowry Box*. (126, Roy's italics)

The use of the word "edifying" is a scathing comment of the author on the cheapening and the loss of India's riches to cater to the demands of indifferent and rich Western tourists. This is in the vein of Ziauddin Sardar's criticism of the erasure of the various cultures of poorer or formerly colonised countries which are reduced to empty objects of consumerism.

> When non-western cultural artefacts appear in the west, they do so strictly as ethnic chic or empty symbols.[5]

The remaining paragraphs dedicated to the description of the touristic services offered are a fierce onslaught on the cheapened sale of cultural treasures to a barely informed and interested western consumer as Sardar points out: "It is not experiential; it does not transform our perceptions; it does not reach out and stir our soul: it entertains, focuses our attention on the spectacle for a fleeting moment and then move on. Under such circumstances, Other ['Other' being Eastern] cultures are seen as articulate objects."[6]

We thus have another intentional use of topicalisation that explains, in the eyes of the narrator, the reasons of this cultural massacre, taking for example the Kathakali performances: "'Small attention spans,' the Hotel People explained to the dancers." (127)

The performances, which are a way of life to the dancers, as well as being fundamental religious and cultural references, become background entertainment to tourists busy sunbathing. This places side-by-side two worlds that were not meant to be thus paired, as one is the core of a country's culture and the other is mere relaxing of tourists uncaring and ignorant of the value of the cultural spectacle they are offered. "While Kunti revealed her secret to Karna on the river bank, courting couples rubbed suntan oil on each other." (127) Roy's comment on the sale and particularly the cheapening of her culture can hardly be missed here.

Similar to italics, one-word sentences obviously meant to lay emphasis on the word and the meaning, the importance of its meaning in the story. The most revealing one-word sentences are those that underline the events that lead to the main tragedy, and they concern the socially condemnable sexual relation between a high-case woman and an 'Untouchable.' Velutha's love-making with Ammu is thus represented as a desecration, reflecting the common attitude toward the Dalits, particularly as the evocation of Velutha's feelings for Ammu are placed in a second position by the narrator:

> "Entered."
> "Loved." (78)

The very next page contains another reprehensible act by Velutha, thus revealing to what extent he was considered as a danger to the order of things and explaining why all leagued against him until he was trapped and killed: his combat for, and it is "Marching" (79). He is part of the disfavoured Communists who believed in the Party and thus fought to better their condition.

An extremely important one-word sentence is the one that the narrator chooses to place at the very end of the novel is "Tomorrow" (340). This position of the word stresses the criminality of the caste system and the tragedy that resulted from it as the reader is confronted with the reason for Velutha's death, which is opposed to the beauty of what the lovers shared. The word is also meant to place hope in a change concerning the situation of the Dalits, by pushing back with a single word, in this novel's non-linear narration, the worst events and leaving the promise of encounter between the lovers as the last impression on the reader's mind.

Incomplete or subject-less sentences are meant to convey the unsaid but shared knowledge between the reader and the narrator concerning social or moral values. Often, it is a comment on the upturning of these values by "polite society." For instance, "As for Rahel" (15) is an obviously incomplete sentence and seems to convey the rumours behind the incomplete sentence. It indicates the moral condemnation she would have faced had it been a morally righteous person who related her past. It ironically mimics Baby Kochamma's choice of remaining "quiveringly silent" upon the case of divorced women from intercommunity love marriages (46).

The incomplete sentences "Not when Mammachi died. Not when Chacko emigrated to Canada" (18) when read alone, reinforce the emotional bond that links the twins, which the reader had been presented with their quasi-biological oneness on the second page of the novel and therefore reveal the sole link that ties Rahel to Ayemenem and explains her presence there, that is the return of her brother Esthappen.

- **India-isms: Syntaxical Deviation, Faulty Spellings and Coining**

The device of faulty spellings is used not only to render the Indian accent at times, but also to make a sarcastic comment on the attitudes of certain characters such as the spelling of the word "divorce," "Die-vorced," which holds in it the condemning attitude of "good" society towards a divorced woman. Not only has Rahel socially committed suicide by divorcing, indicated in "Die," but the probable reasons to this divorce as per Comrade Pillai are also enclosed in the form of the word, which would be her barrenness, "Die" after all, meaning that there is no "issue" or child from her former marriage. The question of Rahel leaving her husband never occurs to him as he is of the old order. What other way to ridicule his attitude than the narrator's attributing to him not only a high-perched voice but also a peculiar pronunciation that mocks his "principles."

Likewise, Comrade Pillai resorts to bookish language when he needs to promote his interests or to confer importance on ordinary events when he wishes to underline their significance. Some of his uses of English are peculiar and remind one of the fact that learning a foreign language or even a second out of context can sometimes give rise to strange uses. The most absurd and hilarious example of the peculiar English or 'India-isms' in order to display mastery of the language of the 'coloniser' or late ruler being, "My sister Sudha met with fracture sometime back" (274). Indians are familiar with Indian actors turning to English in some films when they are angry! English is the showing-off language, for displaying knowledge, power and social status. Lenin acquires social position through his partial mastery of the English language. The profession and the material belongings that he can boast of, are an accurate reflection of how far a person can go in Indian society today by the evaluation of his mastery of English. English is still very much the means to acquire social status in India. This is why Rahel, Chacko, and the twins' father can go abroad to make a living.

Within the anglophile family, English is, of course, used as a means of battling for authority as the mastery of the language gives its speaker at least the impression of belonging to those who rule the world. Ammu's witticism on Chacko's pompous statement on 'coming down' from Oxford after reading there, is delivered by the narrator like a lesson. The letters "a" and "b" are used to classify his enumeration, in an apt summing up of Chacko's pompousness and dreams of status that totally mismatch his abilities. Ammu's use of English and her use of her abilities is a far more practical one as in her teaching her children to be polite or in her giving them the love that children need, "Goodnight Godbless." Their use of the language mirrors their real roles in the family, Ammu helps nourish the family while Chacko, with his Balliol oar exhibited in the factory as a proof of his education and his ownership of the enterprise, brings down everything that the women build just as his planes regularly crash.

> Chacko said: You don't go to Oxford. You read at Oxford. And. (b) After reading at Oxford you come down. 'Down to earth, d'you mean?' Ammu would ask. That you definitely do. Like your famous airplanes. Ammu said that the sad but entirely predictable fate of Chacko's airplanes was an impartial measure of his abilities. (56)

There is more than wrangling to these frequent (as the use of "would" indicates) verbal exchanges between the brother and the sister, for Ammu is bitterly commenting upon the unfairness of the system which privileges a man over a woman without taking their work into consideration (57). Her witticism on the word "down" is also an indicator of the higher classes' unthinking mimicry of the British symbolised in Chacko's insistence on trying to succeed in the flying of his mini aircrafts of the clearly defective kits that he receives presumably from England.

The witticism of Ammu is found in the twins' use of the English language who have been nurtured on English literature by their family. The cleverness of Estha's use of adult language and his delighting in it, clearly appears in his use of the words that are capitalised, "a Highly Stupid Impression" (60), to describe Miss Mitten's error concerning the language spoken in Kerala. The capitalising of the words here indicates the tone that a seven-year-old would probably adopt when parodying adults and underlines the precocious knowledge that enables him to play with the language in such a manner.

On the contrary, Baby Kochamma is a blind consumer of the Western canon and needs to point out to Margaret Kochamma that their family is part of those who collaborated with the highest representatives of English colonialism by quoting Shakespeare. This is why she spends a week eavesdropping on the twins' conversations and especially punishing them as though they were in a classroom so that they use English even in their everyday lives. This use of language as a means of exerting power is indeed confirmed in the punishment the twins receive from their aunt (60), when Miss Mitten complains to her friend Baby Kochamma about their reading backwards. Baby Kochamma imposes fines that are deducted from the twins' pocket money. This can also be compared to the coloniser's rewarding those of the colonised who adapt to his language, culture, whole system, with a livelihood, and sometimes unthinkingly punishes them for having initiative or being independent as in the case of the reading backwards punishment.

Baby Kochamma eavesdrops on the twins' conversations and makes them write hundreds of lines that they will always speak English. It is a symbolic instance of the blind upkeep of some inherited practices by certain members of the generation closest to the period of the British rule. Baby Kochamma is the guardian of traditions along with Kochu Maria and a number of other characters as seen before. She thus relentlessly checks on the twins as they are part of the new generation which with its permissiveness and hybrid quality through intercommunity marriages is a factor of dreaded change. Baby Kochamma wishes to punish Ammu for rebelling against the laws that prevent her from inheriting like her brother, and in this, she is continuing the efforts of the English who changed certain laws and aspects of life in Kerala. Before the English intervention, it was through women that the inheritance of the lands passed. This upholding of the English laws goes along with the other ancient Hindu laws that do not recognise the right for a woman to anything in her father's home as she takes with her, her share in the dowry.

(b) English 'Credentials' and Ayemenem Royalty

The family is certainly one with a social and economic position in Ayemenem. In addition to this, there is the self-consciousness of the members about their social status and the Dos and Don'ts that accompany it. This class-consciousness is felt and lived in a different way by the characters. For Ammu, it is behaviour, and as developed below, a certain pronunciation that is equally found in English, where class and region can be traced from the accent. This consciousness is evident in Ammu's reprimanding her children when they imitate their father's blowing spit-bubbles. "According to Ammu, only clerks behaved like that, not aristocrats" (84). Therefore, despite her rebelliousness and her relation with a Dalit, she does classify people to a certain extent according to their behaviour, attributing "vulgar" behaviour to 'lower classes' like Inspector Mathews who speaks a coarse variant of the Malayalee dialect, and refined behaviour to aristocrats.

For the other members of the family, the mastery of English is a mark of distinction from the masses. The entire family is described by Ammu as an anglophile one, with certain members of it being particularly subservient to the memory of England. English is the criterion of classification of certain people for baby, and Chacko resorts to quoting passages in English in his "Reading Aloud voice" when he is in his "Oxford Moods" (54).

Through Chacko's eyes, England resumes its powerful position and thus reasserts the English superiority in his still colonised mind for he is even thankful to Margaret Kochamma for divorcing him, a slothful 'aristocratic' husband for a practical, working Englishman. Chacko certainly plays the role of the ingratiating weak rulers of India who first allowed the country come under English power through the first agreements and military aid to chain their own people. Indeed, Chacko's using of a machine, which represents Western technology as opposed to his mother's ancient ways, to run the factory along modern financial rules, only brings it to its knees, symbolically representing India's surrender to the colonisers. Like his father, he has taken only the external appearances of the English. For if Pappachi was in fact an ex-high-ranking Government official under the British, his very function "Imperial Entomologist" changed to Joint Director, Entomology" (48-49) is devoid of any concrete outcome as the moth that he discovers is at first not even recognised and then named after a junior officer that he loathes.

The meaninglessness of his attire and the symbol of his acculturation are underlined by the word "sight" that I highlight in the quote below as though he were an exhibition of a useless relic of the past similar to his new designation after independence. He is 'Joint Director' and the young officer after whom the moth is named is "Acting" Director of the Department, and this curiously reminds us of an opposite, where his wife who created and runs the pickle factory is named "Sleeping Partner" while Chacko the hopeless failure "runs" the business. He is the emblem of the Brown Sahib acquiring the outward appurtenances of the ruler and being totally out of connection with his own environment as revealed by his clothes and his car which are totally unsuitable for the weather and the area.

> He bought the skyblue Plymouth from an old Englishman in Munnar. He became a familiar *sight* in Ayemenem, coasting importantly down the narrow road in his wide car, looking outwardly elegant but sweating freely inside his woollen suits. (48)

Likewise, significantly, the picture that is exhibited in the drawing room has been taken in Vienna and moreover he wears jodhpurs like the English even though the reader is informed that he never rode a horse in his life. Father and son expose as a sign of their superiority what the "ruler race" has bestowed upon them. Chacko too has his Balliol oars hung up in the factory and his Oxford education does not help him very much in the running of the factory. What better exemplification could there be of father and son's colonised state of mind when the father refused to believe his daughter's complaint "simply because he didn't believe that an Englishman, *any* Englishman, would covet another man's wife" (42), and Chacko at different points reveals his pride in having been married to an English woman? Father and son are thus a typical example of the Englishman's winning bet on remodelling the native's mind so that he is convinced of the coloniser's superiority.

> The natives must either be kept down by a sense of our power or they must willingly submit from a conviction that we are more wise, more just, more humane and more anxious to improve their condition than any other rulers they could have.[7]

Through his comparison of earth to a woman and the history to an old house at night, Chacko has in fact pickled the history of Kerala and even of the third world. Therefore, the following generation sees it in the same way as the English see it. In addition, he underlines the lack of importance of individuals' lives in the face of History. His relation to the English language is obsessive and servile as he teaches the language to the twins through constant reference to the Oxford dictionary, thus revealing how much his knowledge is but an accumulation of what England has bestowed upon India, amongst which, are books of English literature lined in his room. His aimless life is interspersed with disconnected quotes from the novels he has read, memories of an English culture he has learned and admired and that he probably dreamily links to his years spent in England. In this, Chacko is indeed the ideal Brown Sahib of Macaulay's project, able only to mimic but helpless and hopeless when he actually ventures into applying whatever knowledge he has obtained in his life and work. No wonder that he who taught the twins about perspective sorely lacks it at the time he could have done with some detachment (53).

Baby Kochamma having since long known her superiority to other Indians through her comparison of her English with the other novices' English in the convent. Now aged, she still needs to compare herself to the British. So, when Margaret Kochamma arrives from England, she is unable to restrain herself and starts off by stating that most of the people who are waiting in the airport lounge are "Sweeper Class." This need to place herself above other Indians, which would mean closer to the top of the pyramid where the English are situated in her mind, makes her unable to distinguish between children and adults. She insistently quotes Shakespeare to Sophie Mol (144) believing the nine-year-old child to be learned in the classics. The irony is that the children that she punishes whenever they lapse into Malayalam are more educated than her adult friends who come to educate the twins. Miss Mitten, Baby's Australian missionary friend, is so rigid in her ways that she neither understands nor appreciates palindromes when she is taught them by the children. Moreover she has set views about the level of education in third world countries and brings the twins a baby book that is way below their interests and competence. When they display their quick-wittedness by reading it backwards fluently, she can only react like an uneducated, superstitious bigot as she believes that the practice is evil and declares she has seen Satan in the twins' eyes. Miss Mitten has never heard about palindromes while the seven-year-old twins practise it fluently. This is apparently a *clin d'œil* to those who are fed up of getting the worn views of the world media on the backward, traditional, superstitious East and the modern and rational West and a little jibe at the ordinary westerner who equates superstitions with the so-called third world.

The male character's learning or diplomas are ridiculed. That Chacko is declared to be made of Prime Ministerial stuff is a mockery, for the reader is shown in less than a page that he cannot even run a factory and leads the family into bankruptcy. His hanging his Balliol oars in a pickle factory is ludicrous and his "Reading Aloud" voice and Oxford moods are shown as symptomatic of a man living out of reality, engaged in pursuing women while those over whom he reigns and lords, Velutha, Mammachi, Ammu, work hard and keep a roof over his head. He is intent on asserting his position as such when he informs the twins that everything from the house to the factory belongs to him. Chacko exemplifies a decaying Indian past held in place by the general lack of interest in new ideas, in fact, the fear of them.

Disturbingly, the narrator whose tale is filtered through Rahel's eyes seems to makes an unconscious class distinction. When the narrator allows Rahel's perception to colour the language, through the use of the word "coarse" to describe the Inspector's Malayalam when he sexually humiliates Ammu in the police station, we understand that the Ipe family speaks the genteel version of Malayalam. Through the description of the Inspector's coarse variety of Malayalam we understand that his treatment of Velutha can be turned against him and that the narrator wishes to reveal that if he places himself above Velutha, he is also inferior to someone else and is not to boast about his position. Even if this bias in presentation of the scene can be understood as a reflection of Rahel's pain at this memory, it however perpetrates the hierarchical system. It places the Inspector on a lower level because of his belonging to a lower class and not only because of his rude behaviour, as the term "coarse" is applied to the dialect that he speaks. The very social norms that the narrator criticizes are used as the means to value people in the world of the novel, indicating that the test of the *Shibboleth* is still in practice.

Baby Kochamma's use of English is not only ridiculed, but it is also masterfully linked to her empty life through the echoes or repetitions that form an essential characteristic of the novel. Indeed, in the attribution of the word "pronunciation" to Baby Kochamma, the spelling is divided into syllables, "Prer Nun Sea ayshun" (154) containing not only her condition as an ex-nun, but also a cruel comment on the uselessness of her sacrifice. Baby Kochamma had resorted to nunnery in order to live her passion for Father Mulligan who, the female narrator ironically reports, had not only converted to Hinduism but also become closer to other women, a "sea of boiled eggs," reminding us of nuns, read, 'a sea of nuns,' thus claimed forever from Baby's attentions until his death.

Finally, after reading the novel, one understands to what extent it is the bourgeois pretensions of the two men which had brought down the hard work of the two women who had earned the family's living. Indeed, both the father and Chacko, the son, dreamt of being the *crème de Ayemenem,* so to speak. The father, symbolically bought an old car from an Englishman, as though taking over the authority and position of the coloniser, but the car is useless for want of activity on his part until after his death and his son's departure it ends up stuck in the ground, "Like an angular, arthritic hen [. . .] with no intention of ever getting up" (295). Similarly, the son, puts up a fancy sign, while he does not participate in the actual pickling work and the signboard shares the fate of the car, "rotted and [fallen] inwards like a collapsed crown" (295). Thus, the two elements that the important male figures of the family greatly affect as symbols of their belonging to the ruling class and caste ironically become the means by which their psychological collapse and economic failure are measured.

3. Voices/Voicelessness

The question of voices is central to the novel, as it is about the right to speak and appropriate space, living space through one's ability to speak. For a thorough analysis of the importance of voices and silencing in the novel see Vanessa Guignery's article that explores the polyphonic criss-cross of voices which weaves different sub-stories into the main narrative. Guignery's reading of the novel detects the hints that the narrator drops for the reader to pay attention to the reasons why the characters switch from one language to another, from one tone of voice to a specific kind of silence.[8]

(a) Re-Writing 'Official' History

The right to a recognised space even to a hybrid, an 'outcast' is defended by the narrator through the inventive use of the English language. Of course the particular Indian use of the English language is already known through the example of Salman Rushdie. Yet, the undeniable uniqueness of Roy's use of English in the novel comes in her use of a child's interpretation and understanding of the language. Through the children's perception and using the words, the adults crawling in front of representatives of the white English-speaking world are thoroughly mocked. English is more than an imitation, or even an appropriation of the coloniser's language as the twins' language shows. The language becomes an enriching space in which meaning lives, as the children feel and understand, and they are not yet totally moulded into a certain shape by their environment. This is why the "children's" re-writing of their history and of Kerala's history takes on a new meaning, for it rejects adult interpretations. It suffuses wasted concepts of liberty, honesty, jealousy, love and romanticism through the twins' experiences of life and nature and is narrated in the most direct manner.

The first instance of setting right a part of the story appears at the very beginning of the novel, when Rahel's return to Ayemenen will erase a part of the falseness of what was recorded on Estha's mind. He had lost his ability to speak because he had pronounced a single word that was to make a villain of his beloved friend Velutha in the eyes of all. He had then adopted Baby Kochamma's history that he and his sister were responsible for and guilty of the tragic turn of the events. This continuous self-accusation which had pushed him into silence twenty three years before, is going to be erased by Rahel who, by her presence, will do her best to reveal the truth and the world as it is to him. "The world, locked out for years, suddenly flooded in, and now Estha couldn't hear himself for the noise." (15)

(b) Silencing and Erasure

The narrator's mentioning of the female workers of the factory is limited to the description of their giggling like silly adolescents, notwithstanding their married condition. Equally there is a brief mention of Chacko's daydreaming about his pseudo-Marxist consultations with the prettiest workers rather dwarves the presence of these labourers who are greater in number than Velutha and who exist all through the novel. This seems to be an instance of the middle-class or high-class woman writer in India who dwells on the psychological misery of her class while ignoring the real sufferings of the women of the lower classes and of the rural areas. However, Roy never asserted that she was writing a social or a political pamphlet. It is primarily the story of the twins and their family. Her very style, with the short dry sentences can be said to evoke a large number of problems, sub-stories in a dense and efficient manner, thus giving her few allusions a stronger impact than if she had dwelled on this aspect. The novel is indeed brimming with little stories competing for attention and the result is a little wonder, so one cannot ask for more than the thousand and one stories she has very ably narrated in a single work. The novel is not focused on the sole tribulations of a middle-class family, but evokes a host of issues from the Dalits, to those depending on tourism for their meagre living, to the environment around the characters. The author's allusion here is of course to the discriminatory laws that her own mother had faced and fought and which do not allow a woman to inherit as her brother, which explains why Chacko can chase his sister from her own parents' home after the tragedy. The events leave an aridity in Estha's mind where silence takes over and reflects the end of his living as "the dry season looked as though it would last forever" (10). This leads us to the question of voice.

The position that people occupy enables them to speak or silences them along with their personal tragedies. The weight of the twins' loss that cannot be mourned and forgotten, as all the events are hushed for fear of a scandal, "Silence hung in the air like a *secret* loss" (91, my italics). To acknowledge the importance of their loss would be to reveal the cracks in the official history. When the twins realise that what they are witnessing is some perverted form of the application of law as they wonder why the policemen have brought Velutha behind the History House to punish him for an unexplained crime, they silence themselves, "Screams died in them and floated belly up" (308). The greater physical impact seems to be in Estha, for while continuing to live, Rahel is filled with emptiness, but Estha is filled with silence, "Silence slipped in like a bolt" (320). His sense of guilt leaves him living in memories, unable to move forward. This attitude is summarised in two one-words sentences underlying the finality of his state, "Unspeakable. Numb" (12), and in general revealing in him a complete withdrawal from the world.

Likewise, when their mother has to bow to the stronger, it is her voice, and not her, that is made to agree even though she does not clearly position herself on the side of the keepers of tradition, "Maybe they're right, Ammu's *whisper* said" (302, my italics).

When the members of the minority groups express themselves, the result is doubly farcical as with the reciting of Lenin or his cousin Latha (271-75). First, the poems that both children recite are not understood by themselves and reveal a blind imitation of the members of higher-class which therefore reinforces the position of the latter even though there is a struggle for power between the landed aristocrats and the Communists (275). Secondly, it reveals in which context the landed and the powerful are disposed to listen to the poor: when they parody them without contesting their position. The parallel can be drawn with Kalyani, who apparently understands some English but does not utter a word, only smiling her agreement with her husband (278).

On the other hand, erasure mostly occurs with women who oppose the order and refuse the limited role of wife and mother. Ammu, who disagrees with most figures of authority, be they male or female, is finally silenced as she is chased to the margins of society until she dies a lonely death in a cheap hotel. Ammu's ostracism is complete as she is deprived even of the presence of her own children in her last moments.

> Ammu died in a grimy room in the Bharat Lodge in Allepey, . . . She died alone. With a noisy ceiling fan for company and no Estha to lie at the back of her and talk to her. (161)

Ammu is even physically erased as she is incinerated and in fact even the receipt that Rahel collects from the crematorium does not ascertain that the corresponding jar does indeed contain her mother's ashes, symbolically paralleling the extent to which the traditional society will go to obliterate a woman who has not respected the rules.

Thus, the revealing of the voice and the voicelessness of the various characters reflects the narrator/ Rahel's wish to reconstitute the story and unearth the buried version.

NOTES

1. Homi K. Bhabha, *The Location of Culture* (1994; London: Routledge, 1995), p. 86.
2. For an analysis of Roy's complex treatment of the East-West theme in her novel, see Catherine Pesso-Miquel, "'Queen Cigars' and 'Peppermint Children': Foreign Arrivals in *The God of Small Things*," Jean-Pierre and Carole Durix, "Reading Arundhati Roy's *The God of Small Things*." (Collection U21. Editions Universitaires de Dijon, 2002).
3. See my development on 'locusts stand I' under the sub-title 'female creativity or textual domination?'
4. Rodney Huddleston, *Introduction to the Grammar of English* (Cambridge University Press, 1984), pp. 454-56.
5. Ziauddin Sardar, *Postmodernism and the Other. The New Imperialism of Western Culture* (London: Pluto Press, 1998).
6. *Ibid.*, p. 134.
7. "Minute of J. Farsh," 28.8.1938. Qtd. B.K. Boman-Behran, *Educational Controversies of India: The Cultural Conquest of India under British Imperialism* (Bombay: Taraporevala, 1942), p. 239. Cf. Tharu and Lalitha, Vol. II, p. 10.
8. Vanessa Guignery, "Le Spectre des Voix dans *The God of Small Things*," in François Gallix, "Arundhati Roy: *The God of Small Things—L'hybridité célébrée*." (Paris: Mallard Éditions. Collection Angloscopies, 2002).

Conclusion

The autobiographical elements of the novel, which one would tend to turn to can be considered as the author does not hide its presence. However, it is the artistic creation that won the novel its prize and that is what should be kept in mind. Roy's novel represents a watershed in the Indian literary scene, as it is the first novel written by a female author, unknown to top it all, to win the Booker Prize. A welcome recognition probably but not considered as a passport to the West for the author has firmly declared that she will always remain in India, through no excessive nationalism, but just because she is comfortable in her own world that she doesn't seem to wish to exchange for other skies. While the novel clearly celebrates the English language through its playful approach to it, the female narrator who clearly values her culture and language, frowns upon excessive Anglophilia, especially accompanying the self-deprecation of the formerly colonised.

Arundhati Roy's novel is one that explores the struggles of the minority groups and attempts to relate their stories from the point of view of an even less visible group in fiction, children. In this polyphonic text, the reader is reminded at multiple times that history can be fictionalised, that truth is an amorphous concept, and that a single story can turn out to be multi-faceted, multi-layered as it has several actors, voices. The main issue is caste and the man-woman relationship, yet other issues such as globalisation or frontier wars are woven into the main narrative. Thus from the personal journeys of Ammu, Velutha, Rahel and Estha, the reader can move to the larger issues making the novel's meanings seem nearly endless.

Glossary and Cultural References Guide

Vocabulary and Cultural Allusions

Addeham: respectful form of "he"

Ajantha: The brand name of an audio equipment company in Kerala, named after the famous Buddhist cave site.

Aiyyo: What a pity! How sad! An expression of self lament depending on context.

Aiyyo kashtam: Literally, "Oh, what a pity!" but used here as a reproach: "How could you say that?" (*Kashtam*: pain, suffering)

Aiyyo, Mon! Mol!: Oh dear! Boy! Girl! Or also, Son! Daughter! Kuttappen is embarrassed at the children having heard him shout out his scatological song (208).

Aiyyo paavam: 'Poor thing' here.

Allay edi: Isn't that so? (rude)

Amhoo: Moo.

Ammai: wife of mother's brother

Ammaven: Uncle: the mother's brother.

Ammooma's: Grandmother's.

Anthurium andraeanum: A large, waxy flower which originated in Colombia, but which is now common in Hawaii and other tropical locales. The most popular varieties are red "rubrum."

Appoi: Mother's brother

Appoopan's: Grandfather's.

Ashram: Hindu spiritual centre.

Avial: A spicy vegetable stew cooked in coconut milk, a typical Malayali dish.

Avalose oondas: balls of sweetened pressed rice.

Ayurvedic: Traditional Indian medicine.

Baba: Man. The word is used for any elder person (male) in the family holding a position of authority: elder brother, father.

Bandh: General strike used as a political protest.

Betel: The chewing of betel leaf causes the saliva to turn red.

Bhajan: A devotional song.

Bindis: A red dot worn on the forehead by married women.

Burning ghat: Funeral pyre.

Cannae and phlox Canna indica: originated in tropical America, but has been commonly cultivated in England, under the name "Indian shot." None of these flowers is native to India.

Chachen: Father.

Chacko Saar vannu: Mr. Chacko has arrived. "Saar" is a phonetic spelling of an Indian pronunciation of the English word "Sir."

Chakka Velaichathu: Jackfruit jam.

Chappu Thamburan: A spider.

chatta: Blouse.

cheduthi: older brother's wife.

Chenda: Drum.

Chetan: Older brother.

chhi-chhi: Children's language for excrement, used as an expression of disgust.

Churidar: Traditional narrow, tight-fitting trousers with folds near the ankles, worn by both men and women in North India.

DDA flat: Delhi Development Authority apartment.

Dhobi: Person who washes clothes for a living.

Diwali: The very popular fall Hindu festival of lights. Also known as "Deepavali."

eda cherrukka!: hey you, boy!

Edi: hey, you! The suffixes "di" and "da" used respectively for women and men in Malayalam can indicate either intimacy or a social/age based inferiority.

Enda?: What is it?

Ende Deivomay! My God!

EEE sadhanangal!: All these things!

Fresh tandoori pomfret: Fish baked in a traditional clay oven.

Government benefits: The Indian government has engaged in strenuous affirmative action on behalf of untouchables ever since independence, but these measures have not reached all of them.

Gram: Lentil.

Idli appams: Steamed, rice string hoppers coconut, sugar and other ingredients may be added for taste, but do not form part of the appam as such.

"*Inquilab*": 'Revolution' from the Arabic verb "inkalaba": to revolt.

Inquilab Zindabad!: Long live the Revolution!

Ividay!: Over here!

Jackfruits: A very large sweet fruit common in South and East Asia.

Kando, Kochu Mariye?: "'Can you see her Kochu Mariye?.'

Kandoo, Kochamma: 'I can see her Kochamma.'

Kanji: Rice water.

Kappa: Tapioca. Cassava root, cooked in various ways.

Kashtam: suffering.

Kavani: Top part of a two-piece sari, draped diagonally across the upper body.

Kebabs: Spiced, marinated meat, ground or in cubes, usually grilled on a skewer.

Keto!: listen!

Keto: Have you heard?

"Thanks, keto!," "Valarey thanks.": "Thanks a lot, all right?"

Kodam puli tree: A variety of tamarind tree bearing fruit shaped like a *kodam* or round bowl.

Koh-i-noor: An enormous diamond now part of the crown jewels of England; but it originally belonged to the Mughals, Muslim rulers of India.

Kohl: Black eyeliner, used to darken the inner rim of the eyelid. A word derived from Arabic.

Koojah: Earthenware water jar.

Koshy Oommen: A typical Syrian Christian name.

Kunukku earrings: A type of ancient Christian Keralite jewellery, usually gold earrings consisting of a short, thin chain with a small ball hanging from it.

Kushumbi: Jealous woman or girl.

Kuthambalam: Inner part of the Hindu temple, just outside of the inner sanctum.

Kutty: little, small, used for a little girl.

Laddoo: A common sort of cookie made of lentil flour, ghee, raisins, nuts, and spices.

Little Nehru: Dressed like the first premier of India, Jawaharlal Nehru.

Madiyo?: Is it enough?

Madi aaririkkum: It may be enough.

Maharani: Queen.

Malayala Manorama: Kerala's largest circulating Malayalam daily newspaper.

Mandalay: In central Burma.

Mango hair: Mangoes contain fibres which easily get caught between the teeth.

Mangosteen Garcinia mangosiana: A tropical fruit with a thick, dark-red skin.

Mammachi: Grandmother.

Mariakutty: Little Maria.

Meen: Fish.

Meeshas: Moustaches.

Mittam: Yard.

Modalali: Landlord

Mol!: Little girl! or Daughter depending on context.

Mon!: Little boy! Or Son depending on context.

Mundu: A single piece of cloth arranged tied at the waist, worn by both men and women.

Naach: dance

Naaley: tomorrow.

Namaste: Traditional Indian gesture of greeting, palms together and upright.

Onam: Harvest festival of Kerala celebrated during ten days in the month of August/ September. Since 1882, boat races are a regular feature of this festival in Kottayam.

Onner Runder Moonner: One, two, three.

Ooty cupboards: Ooty is the popular name of Udhagamandalam, a luxurious "hill station" in the Nilgiri Mountains of Tamil Nadu, just across the border from Kerala in the northeast. Furniture from there would have belonged to wealthy people.

Oower: Yes.

Orkunnilley: Don't you remember?

Oru kaaryam parayettey?: Shall I tell you something?

Pallu: The loose end of a sari which is draped over the shoulder.

Pappachi: Grandfather

Paratha: Fried flat bread, often stuffed with spiced vegetables, and generally an unsuitable companion to chocolate sauce.

Paravan: An Untouchable caste name.

Pariah: Untouchable.

parippu vadas: Also vadai: spicy fried patties made of ground lentils. A common street food.

Parippu: lentils

Parsis Zoroastrians: called "Farsis" from the Arabic word, *Farisi*, in Persia, Iran. They have only small communities in India, necessarily somewhat inbred.

Peetika: colophon

Po: Go rude).

Poda Patti! Get lost, you dog!

PWD: Public Works Department.

Rakshasa: Demon.

Saar: Malayali pronunciation of "sir."

Sadhus: Hindu ascetics.

In saffron: In saffron-yellow robes, traditionally worn by holy men.

Shervani: "Nehru jacket": long formal jacket with a stand-up collar.

Soo-soos: Children's word for penis, somewhat like 'tiddler.'

Sundari kutty: Beautiful little girl.

Sundari: beautiful; *Kutty*: small, little girl here.

Swami(s): Senior member(s) of a Hindu religious order.

Sweeper class: Members of an untouchable caste.

Tiffin carrier: Tiffin (U.K.): a light midday meal. Tiffin carriers are lunchboxes usually made of stainless steel in India.

Thozhilali: worker, labourer.

Toddy tapper: Toddy is the sweet, fermented sap of various palm trees, tapped to provide a cheap alcoholic drink.

Valarey: name used for an important person.

Vallom: Boat.

Vannu: has arrived.

Vellya Paapen: Old uncle.

Velliya: big, strong.

Veshya: Prostitute.

Vevichatu: Cooked.

Zamindar: landowner who had the obligation to pay a huge tax on his revenues and therefore exploited the peasants.

Names and Associations Linked to Them

The Vedic Rishis, sages, of India believed that a child's name influenced his face, body, character, personality, morality and profession. Names and the associations linked to them are therefore important in India. Even in the case of such a novel where the names of the major characters are Christian certain aspects of Indian culture underline the social roles attached to them as is the case for the suffixes attached to the names. The suffixes "*appa*," "father," and "*amma*", "mother" are typical of Tamil Nadu and the Karnataka. A girl is a potential mother and therefore many Indian female names have the suffix « amma » attached to them, as in the twins' grandmother's name, Sosha, becomes Soshamma, or Paravati, Paravtiamma. Sometimes the suffix "Devi" meaning "Goddess" is also attached to a girl's name, as in Mahadevi, or Laxmidevi. In the novel, "kutty," "small," a typically Malayalee suffix. For boys the suffix "appa," "appen," "father" is attached to the name as in "Kuttappen," Velutha's elder brother, is "Mounniappa," or "Swamy" which is a title for a senior member of a Hindu religious order, as in "Govindaswamy." None of the characters has a name from the Hindu Gods or Goddesses.

Ammu means "love" in Malayalam, "kutty" means little or small, "Ammukutty," means "little love."

Esthappen: Stephen: first Christian martyr (celebrated on December 26), stoned to death (Acts, 6, 7).

Kalyani: Comrade Pillai's wife, from the Sanskrit (Kalyanin is the masculine form): (1) beneficial; (2) lucky; excellent; propitious; a sacred cow; (3) a follower of Skanda (M. Bh = Mahabharata); a ragini; Dakshayani in Malaya (M. Bh); another name for Parvati; Indian Senna Cassia (augustifolia); Terramnus labialis.[2]

Rahel: Biblical name from the Hebrew Rachel.

Sosha: a Biblical name. Mother of Jesus in Malayalam.

Velutha means "white" and we know that Velutha is black.

Yako: a Biblical name, a Malayalee variant of Jacob. *Yaakoub* in Arabic.

NOTES

1. The glossary of Malayalam words has been constructed thanks to the Internet site by Paul Brians, "Arundhati Roy: The God of Small Things Study Guide," http://www.wsu.edu:8080/~brians/anglopho ne/roy.html, and to the glossary by Guignery, Vanessa in Gallix, François, Arundhati Roy: *The God of Small Things—L'hybridité célébrée.* Paris: Mallard Éditions. Collection Angloscopies, 2002.
2. Maneka Gandhi, *The Penguin Book of Hindu Names* (1989; Viking Penguin India, 1992), p. 174.

Bibliography

A. Fiction

Roy, Arundhati. *The God of Small Things*, London: Flamingo, 1997.

B. Non-Fiction

Coates Ken, ed. *War is Peace. The Spokesman* (N) 73. Nottingham, UK: Russell Press, 2001.

Roy, Arundhati. *The Cost of Living*, London: Flamingo, 1999.

_____. *Power Politics*. Cambridge, Massachusetts: South End Press, 2001.

_____. "Seize the Time!" In These Times magazine, July 2003. Rep. *International Socialist Review* Issue 38, November-December 2004

_____. "What We Call Peace is Little Better Than Capitulation to a Corporate Coup." *Sydney Morning Herald* (Australia), Wednesday, November 3, 2004.

_____. An interview by Sandip Roy, *Mid-Day*, October 31, 2004

"Finding Justice with Arundhati Roy." Interview by Terrence McNally, AlterNet. Posted September 21, 2004.

_____. "The New American Century," *The Nation*, February 9, 2004

"Scimitars in the Sun," N. Ram interviews Arundhati Roy on a writer's place in politics. Volume 18, Issue 01, Jan. 6-19, 2001 at http://www.the hindu.com/fline/fl1801/index.htm

"Indian Elections and Resistance." Amy Goodman interviews Arundhati Roy, May 19, 2004. Arundhati Roy on the Indian Elections, Her Support for the Iraqi.

Roy, Arundhati. "Resistance and the Privatization of War, India's real and virtual worlds have collided in a humiliation of power," *The Guardian*, Friday May 14, 2004.

_____. *An Ordinary Person's Guide to Empire*, South End Press, 2004

_____. *War Talk*, South End Press, 2003.

_____. "The day of the jackals," June 6, 2003

_____. "Confronting Empire." [Speech Given at World Social Forum January 27, 2003, in Porto Alegre, Brazil]. North Bay Progressive newspaper, Feb. 25-Mar. 25, 2003

_____. Come September (September 18, 2002) *Frontline Magazine*, Volume 19, Issue 20, October 12-25, 2002, India. http://www.doccentre.org/TOD/Roy-come-sept.htm

_____. Mesopotamia. Babylon. The Tigris and Euphrates. http://www.cnn.com

_____. Democracy: Who's She When She's at Home? From *Outlook India* Magazine, 6 May 2002.

_____. Shall We Leave It to the Experts?, *The Nation*, February 18, 2002

_____. Fascism's Firm Footprint in India, The Nation magazine, September 30, 2002

_____. The Algebra of Infinite Justice, The Progressive magazine, December 2001

_____. 'Brutality Smeared in Peanut Butter' by Arundhati Roy

_____. In conversation with Venu Govindu, Oct 29, 2000 at the NBA dharna in Bhopal.

_____. *The Great Indian Rape Trick*, I August 22nd, 1994 September & *The Great Indian Rape-Trick II*, September 3rd, 1994.

Books and Articles

Baneth-Nouailhetas, Emiliene. *The God of Small Things*. Arundhati Roy. Malesherbes: Armand Colin / VUEF-CNED, 2002.

Bhatt, Indira and Indira Nityanandam. *Explorations: Arundhati Roy's The God of Small Things*. New Delhi: Creative, 1999.

Dhawan, R.K., ed. *Arundhati Roy. The Novelist Extraordinary*. New Delhi: Prestige, 1999.

Dodiya, Jaydipsinh and Joya Chakravarty, ed. *The Critical Studies of Arundhati Roy's The God of Small Things*. New Delhi: Atlantic, 2001.

Duperray, Max, ed. *La vérité en littérature*. Aix-en-Provence: Publications de l'Université de Provence, 2002.

Durix, Jean-Pierre and Carole. *Reading Arundhati Roy's The God of Small Things*. Collection U21. Editions Universitaires de Dijon, 2002.

Dwivedi, A.N. and Nath, Amar, ed. *Arundhati Roy's Fictional World. A Collection of Critical Essays*. New Delhi: B.R., 2001.

Gallix. François, Arundhati Roy: *The God of Small Things—L'hybridité célébrée*. Paris: Mallard Éditions. Collection Angloscopies, 2002.

Jha, Surendra Narayan. "Dreams Redreamed: A Study of Arundhati Roy's *The God of Small Things*." *Indian Women Writers*, ed. R.K. Dhawan. New Delhi: Prestige, 2001. 158-71.

Kulkarni, Prahlad A. "From Frustration to Suffering: A Recurring Pattern in Arundhati Roy's *The God of Small Things*." *Indian Women Writers*, ed. R.K. Dhawan. New Delhi: Prestige, 2001. 188-93.

Maiti, Prasenjit. "History and Counterhistory: Reading Novels, Reading Politic: Arundhati Roy's *The God of Small Things*." *Indian Women Writers*, ed. R.K. Dhawan. New Delhi: Prestige, 2001. 145-57.

Misra, Rosy. "The Crisis in Human Values in *Coolie* and *The God of Small Things*: A Comparative Study." *Indian Women Writers*, ed. R.K. Dhawan. New Delhi: Prestige, 2001. 201-9.

Mukherjee, A.K. "Dark of Heartness Tiptoed into the Heart of Darkness: Arundhati Roy's *The God of Small Things*." *Indian Women Writers*, ed. R.K. Dhawan. New Delhi: Prestige, 2001. 194-200.

Mullaney, Julie. *Arundhati Roy's The God of Small Things. A Reader's Guide*. New York, London: Continuum Contemporaries, 2002.

Navarro-Tejero, Antonia. *Gender and Caste in the Anglophone-Indian Novels of Arundhati Roy and Githa Hariharan: Feminist Issues in Cross-Cultural Perspectives*. Edwin Mellen Press, 2005.

Ojha, Uday Shankar and Gajendra Kumar. "*The God of Small Things*: A Novel of Poetic Narraology and Laurentian Ecstasy." *Indian Women Writers*, ed. R.K. Dhawan. New Delhi: Prestige, 2001. 210-17.

Pandey. K.M. "The Small God Made Big: Arundhati Roy's *The God of Small Things*." *Indian Women Writers*, ed. R.K. Dhawan. New Delhi: Prestige, 2001. 172-79.

Pathak, R.S., ed. *The Fictional World of Arundhati Roy*. New Delhi: Creative, 2001.

Prasad, Amar Nath. "Arundhati Roy's 'The Greater Common Good': A Poignant Ode on the Dalit and the Deserted." *Indian Women Writers*, ed. R.K. Dhawan. New Delhi: Prestige, 2001. 218-30.

Saxena, Alka. "Arundhati Roy's *The God of Small Things*: A Study in Abnormal Psychology and Consequent Behaviour Pattern." *Indian Women Writers*, ed. R.K. Dhawan. New Delhi: Prestige, 2001. 138-44.

Sharma, A.P. *The Mind and Art of Arundhati Roy; a Critical Appraisal of Her Novel The God of Small Things*. New Delhi: Minerva Press, 2000.

Sharma, R.S. and Shashi Bala Talwar. *Arundhati Roy's The God of Small Things: Critique and Commentary*. New Delhi: Creative, 1998.

Surendran, K.V. *The God of Small Things. A Saga of Lost Dreams*. New Delhi: Atlantic, 2000.

Verma, Pratibha. "Arundhati Roy's *The God of Small Things*: A Study in Feminine Sensibility and Aspects of Style." *Indian Women Writers*, ed. R.K. Dhawan. New Delhi: Prestige, 2001. 180-87.

Internet pages

http://www.geocities.com/~dvadi/articles/aroy_dbars.html 'Arundhati Roy The Progressive Interview' by David Barsamian.

http://www.wsu.edu:8080/~brians/anglophone/roy.html Paul Brians, "Arundhati Roy: The God of Small Things Study Guide"

http://www.narmada.org/articles/arinterview.html 'Arundhati Roy in conversation with Venu Govindu'. Oct 29, 2000 at the NBA Dharna in Bhopal.

http://www.salon.com/sept97/00roy.html 'The Salon Interview' by Reena Jana, Sept. 30, 1997.

http://www.rediff.com/news/sep/18arun.htm by George Iype 'Rediff on the Net.'

http://website.lineone.net/~jon.simmons/roy/tgodt6c.htm Jon Simmons.

Jaggi, Maya, "An Unsuitable Girl," *Electronic Mail & Guardian. Review of Books*.

Other Works Cited

Bhabha, Homi. K. *The Location of Culture*. London: Routledge, 1995 (1994).

Das, S.K. *A History of Indian Literature. 1911-1956. Struggle for Freedom; Triumph and Tragedy*. New Delhi: Sahitya Akademi, 1995.

Doniger, Wendy and Brian K. Smith, trans. *The Laws of Manu*. New Delhi: Penguin, 1991.

Doniger O'Flaherty, Wendy. *Women, Androgynes and Other Mythical Beasts*. London, Chicago: University of Chicago Press, 1980.

Hanquart-Turner, Evelyne, ed. *Unions Mixtes et Métissages dans le Monde Anglophone*. Publications du CEREC Centre d'études et de recherches sur l'empire et le Commonwealth) de l'Université de Paris XII. Paris: Éditions A3, 1998, p. 35-65.

Huddleston, Rodney, *Introduction to the Grammar of English*. Cambridge University Press, 1984.

Kakar, Sudhir. *Moksha. The Inner World. A Psychoanalytic Study of Childhood and Society in India*. New Delhi: Oxford India Paperbacks, 2002 (1978).

Lal, Malashri. *The Law of the Threshold. Women Writers in Indian English*. Simla: Indian Institute of Advanced Study, 1995.

Lodge, David, *The Art of Fiction*, London: Penguin, 1992.

Mukherjee, Meenakshi. *Realism and Reality, The Novel and Society in India*. Delhi: Oxford University Press, 1985.

Palmer, Paulina. *Contemporary Women's Fiction: Narrative Practice and Feminist Theory*. Hertfordshire: Harvester Wheatsheaf, 1989.

Rao, Raja. *Kanthapura*. New York: New Directions, 1963 (1938).

Reddy, G. Aswathanarayana. *Indian Writing in English & its Audience*. Bareilly: Prakash, 1979.

Rhodes Dusty and Sandra McNeill, ed. *Women against Violence against Women*. Onlywomen Press, 1985, p. 255, qtd. Paulina Palmer.

Sardar, Ziauddin. *Postmodernism and the Other. The New Imperialism of Western Culture*. London: Pluto Press, 1998.

Sibony, Daniel. *Entre-deux l'origine en partage*. Paris: Seuil, 1991.

Tharu, Susie and K. Lalitha, ed. *Women Writing in India. 600 B.C. to the Present*. Vols. I & II. Delhi: Oxford University Press, 1995.

INDEX